10-Minute

♣ CARD ♠

GAMES

William A. Moss
Illustrated by Myron Miller

Sterling Publishing Co., Inc.
New York

To my father, who took time to be a father

Library of Congress Cataloging-in-Publication Data

Moss, William A.
   10-minute card games / William A. Moss.
     p.   cm.
   Includes index.
   ISBN 0-8069-3847-1
   1. Card games. I. Title.
   GV1243.M65   1995
   795.4—dc20

10 9 8 7 6 5

Published by Sterling Publishing Company, Inc.
387 Park Avenue South, New York, N.Y. 10016
© 1995 by William A. Moss
Distributed in Canada by Sterling Publishing
℅ Canadian Manda Group, One Atlantic Avenue, Suite 105
Toronto, Ontario, Canada M6K 3E7
Distributed in Great Britain and Europe by Cassell PLC
Wellington House, 125 Strand, London WC2R 0BB, England
Distributed in Australia by Capricorn Link (Australia) Pty Ltd.
P.O. Box 6651, Baulkham Hills, Business Centre, NSW 2153, Australia
Printed and bound in Hong Kong

Sterling ISBN 0-8069-3847-1

Contents

Introduction 4

The Rummy Group 5

The All Fours Group 12

The Whist Group 17

The Poker Group 21

The Showdown Games Group .34

The Euchre Group 38

The Cassino Group 54

The Hearts Group 59

The Solitaire Group 66

The Stops Group 84

Card Games for Children and the Young at Heart 88

What the Terms Mean 94

Index 96

Introduction

I have long enjoyed playing card games because they have provided me, my family, and friends with wholesome entertainment, camaraderie, and deeper, richer, more meaningful relationships through friendly competition. Hoping, then, to share these benefits with my readers, I have prepared this volume of ten-minute card games.

Why is this book titled *Ten-Minute Card Games*? Simply to remind the reader that most card games require only ten minutes or less to play, and that you do not need large blocks of time for a game once you have learned the rules. Probably all basic card games at first required ten minutes or less to play, but some became more complicated and required longer periods of play in response to players' wanting to prolong the game. For example, over a period of time, Bridge evolved from Whist, Black Lady from the simpler game of Hearts, and a host of other card games from a few basic parent games such as Seven-Up, Rummy, Straight Poker, and others.

My first goal in preparing this book was to offer card games that began as and remained ten-minute games, as well as those that began as ten-minute games but were lengthened somewhat by advanced scoring procedures. In the latter case, I simplified the scoring to return these games to a one-hand, one-game format. However, in each such case I also included the scoring procedure for the higher-score, longer-lasting game for those persons who want to play it. My second goal was to address this book to both men and women, partly because both play cards, and partly out of a sense of fairness. With this goal in mind, I have used both feminine and masculine pronouns throughout the text.

I owe thanks to Margaret, my wife, other family members, friends, and workmates who have played card games with me and encouraged me to prepare my manuscript. I also owe thanks to Sheila Anne Barry of Sterling Publishing Company for her support, without which my efforts would not have reached fruition. Finally, I want to thank Michael Cea, also of Sterling, for his careful editing of my manuscript.

William A. Moss

The Rummy Group

Rummy and its variations originated with the game of *Conquián*, which entered the American Southwest from Mexico during the mid-1800s. Anglo mispronunciation corrupted the name *Conquián* (from *con quién*, meaning "*with whom*") to Cooncan. Other games of Latin origin include Panguingue, Canasta, and Samba.

Basic Rummy, or Rum

Players and Deck Used
Rummy requires from two to six players (four to six being best) and a full 52-card deck. The cards rank from king (high) to ace (low).

Beginning the Game
The players cut for low card (ace being low) to determine first deal and choice of seats. After the shuffle and cut, the dealer deals. In two-hand Rummy, the dealer deals ten cards to each player; in three- or four-hand, seven cards; in five- and six-hand, six cards. The dealer deals the cards one at a time in rotation from left to right. The next card is placed face up beside the *stock* (the portion of the pack of cards *not* dealt to the players), which is put face down near the middle of the table.

The Goal
The goal of the game is to "meld" or lay out all the cards in your hand in sets of three or four of a kind and/or in sequences of three or more cards in the same suit.

The Play
The player to the left of the dealer may either take a card from the top of the stock, without showing it, or take the *discard* (the face-up card next to the stock). He cannot, however, pick up the discard unless he can play it immediately. If he holds three or four cards of the same

5

Ranking of Cards in Basic Rummy

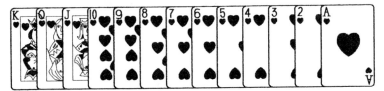

Sequences

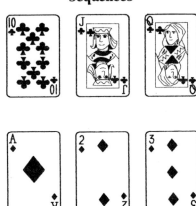

rank, or denomination, or if he holds a sequence of three or more cards in the same suit, he may meld, or lay them out on the table before him. During the same turn at play, he may meld more than one set, if he so wishes. However, he does not *have* to meld on that turn: Some players prefer holding all their melds until they are ready to "go out." But once he has melded or else indicated that he does not wish to meld, he discards one card face up on the pile beside the stock. Each player in rotation to his left has the same opportunity to draw and meld.

Once the game gets under way, a player may, after drawing but before discarding, get rid of one or more cards from his hand by playing them on his own or on other players' melds. For example, if he holds the 6 and 10 of spades, he may play these cards on a spade 7, 8, 9 meld.

If the players exhaust the stock before anyone wins, there are two ways to proceed: (a) Face (turn over) all unplayed cards, declare the holder of such cards with the lowest *pip value* (total count) the winner, and let the other players settle up according to the difference between their pip values. (b) Shuffle and cut the discard pile, and turn it face down to be used again as stock (with its top card turned over as the first discard).

The first person to get rid of all his cards, either laid out as melds or played on the melds of his opponents, wins the game and the next deal. After his last draw, the player who is going out does not have to, but may, discard. At this point, play *ends*, and the other players may *not* play their unplayed cards to other players' melds.

Scoring

The winner collects from each losing player the pip value of his unplayed cards. The cards have the following values: ace, 1 point; 2, 2 points, and so forth through 10; each face card, 10 points. Some players prefer using the following optional values for face cards: jack, 11; queen, 12; king, 13.

Remedies and Penalties

If a person receives too many or too few cards on the deal, he may correct the deal by either returning cards to, or taking cards from, the stock. If a player holds too many cards at the end of the game, the winner scores their pip value. If the player holds too few cards at the end of the game, the winner scores 10 points for each missing card.

If a person lays down cards that are not a valid meld, he can return them to his hand. If such an invalid meld is not discovered until another player has "played off" on it, the played-off cards remain in place. However, the person playing the foul meld cannot go out until he has drawn a card that makes his meld good. If a person plays out of turn and has discarded, the play is valid and the intervening player loses his turn. If a person draws from the stock out of turn but has not discarded, or if he draws two cards by mistake and sees both of them, he places the misdrawn card face up on the stock. The player to whom the misdrawn card should have belonged may either (a) pick up the card and put it in his hand, or (b) bury the card in the stock and draw a replacement card from the top of the stock or from the faced discard pile.

If a person claims to be "out" (that is, he claims he can play all of his cards down and end the game) but is not, he must lay down all melds and play off what cards he can. The game then continues.

Showdown Rummy

In this variation of Basic Rummy, a player holding sets of three or more cards and/or sequences that include every card in her hand may meld her entire hand at any time. Upon melding in this manner, she scores double the pip value of the cards still held in her opponents' hands.

Michigan Rummy

Michigan, another variation of Basic Rummy, also differs from the parent game in five ways:

1. A player may use an ace in a low-end sequence (ace, 2, 3) or in a high-end sequence (ace, king, queen). In the former, the ace is worth 1 point; in the latter, 15 points. Around-the-corner sequences (for example, king, ace, 2) are not permitted.

2. The players overlap their discards in a row so that the rank, or denomination, of each is visible. A player may draw any card from the discard row, but he must be able to play it immediately, and he must also take all the cards above the one he draws.

3. If a player discards a card that he could play on one of his melds, another player may call "Stop!" and thus force him to do so.

4. The player declaring "Rummy" must discard one card. No further melds or playing off is permitted. If a player declares Rummy in error, each opponent scores 20 points for the error.

5. The winner scores the pip value of his opponents' unplayed cards. To win the longer version of the game, the first person to score 500 points wins. If two or more players score more than 500 points in one hand, the higher score wins. A scorekeeper records the running scores with pencil and paper.

Bozenkill Rummy

Bozenkill is a variation of Michigan Rummy. The two games differ in the following respects:

1. Once a player melds a card, she may not use it again in another combination set or sequence.

2. When a person plays a card or cards to an opponent's meld, she does not actually play them to the meld but lays them above her melds, stating to which meld they are played.

3. There are no "Stops."

4. The winner scores the combined pip value of all cards melded in front of her, plus the pip value of all cards left unplayed in each opponent's hand. An opponent's score is the pip value of the cards actually melded by her.

Gin Rummy

This game, usually played by two persons, requires a 52-card deck without the joker. The cards rank as in Basic Rummy: king (high), queen, jack, 10 . . . ace (low). In counting points to determine pip values and scores, each face card is worth 10 points, each ace is worth 1 point, and all other cards are each worth their face, or pip, value.

Ranking of Cards in Gin Rummy

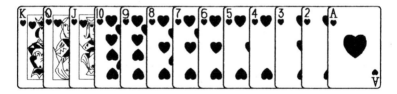

Typical Gin Hand

Beginning the Game

The players cut for high card to determine first deal. High card may choose to deal or to request his opponent to deal. The dealer gives ten cards, one at a time, to each player and puts the 21st card face up beside the stock. Thereafter, the deal passes to the winner of each hand.

The Play

The opponent plays first. He may take or refuse the card put face up by the dealer beside the stock. If he refuses, the dealer may take it; if the dealer also refuses it, the opponent may draw the top card of the stock. Thereafter, each player in turn may take the face card or the top card of the stock, discarding a card in its place. If either player picks up a card from the discard pile, he may not discard it in the same turn at play.

The object of play is to build sets of three or four of a kind and/or sequences of three or more cards in the same suit.

A player may end a hand in one of two ways. First, he may declare "Gin," discard, meld all of his sets and/or sequences at one time, and score the pip, or count, value of his opponent's deadwood (cards that cannot be played as sets and/or sequences) plus 20 points for Gin. Some players prefer 10 points for Gin, while others prefer 25 points. Players should agree on the value of a Gin before play begins.

The second way for a player to end a hand is to knock on the table, thus advising his opponent that he will meld with 10 or fewer points in deadwood, discard, meld his sets and/or sequences, and then expose his unplayable cards. At this point the opponent also lays down what melds he can, and he may, if able, play some or all of his deadwood on the knocker's melds. If the player knocking has less deadwood than his opponent, he scores the difference between the pip values of their deadwood. However, if the opponent holds the same or a lesser amount of deadwood, he scores the difference between the pip values of their deadwood plus 20 (or 10 or 25) points for undercutting the knocker.

If either player holds too few cards after either player has declared Gin or knocked, he is penalized 10 points for each missing card.

If the knocker has more than 10 points' worth of deadwood, the opponent may either accept the knock as valid, or he may require the knocker to continue the play with an exposed hand. In the former case, the player would have one more draw and discard before the knocker would be allowed to close out the play. The knocker, however, may rearrange his cards to justify his claim and preclude a penalty.

If the players run through the stock before either can Gin or knock, one of two remedies may be pursued. First, the players may agree to leave the last discard card face up and then shuffle, cut, and put the other discards face down as stock. Second, the players may agree to abandon their hands without score.

The winner of the hand wins the game. Many Gin enthusiasts, however, prefer playing successive hands (usually two or three) until one player scores 100 points. If the latter procedure is followed, the game will require more than ten minutes of play. If one player scores 100 points before the other player scores any points, the winner is credited with two games instead of one, if such is agreed to at the start of the game. This phenomenon is known variously as a shutout, skunk, whitewash, schneider, etc.

Other Remedies and Penalties
A new deal is required when: (a) a deal out of turn is discovered before the 21st card is put face up; (b) the deck is imperfect; (c) a card is faced in the pack or during the deal; (d) both players hold an incorrect number of cards before or after the first draw; (e) either player holds an incorrect number of cards before or after the first draw, if the person with the correct hand wishes (the correct hand may decide to continue the game and let the other hand, during regular play, draw cards without discarding or discard cards without drawing to attain the correct number of cards).

The All Fours Group

Card players have enjoyed games of the All Fours group, including Seven-Up and its many variations, since the late 1600s. Having its origins in England, Seven-Up, along with Whist and Put, was popular in the early 1700s and for years competed with Poker as the favorite gambling game in the United States.

Seven-Up

Players and Deck Used
The game requires two, three, or four persons (when they are playing as partners, two against two) and a full deck of 52 cards. The cards rank as follows: ace (high), king, queen, jack, 10 . . . 2 (low).

Beginning the Game
The players cut for high card to determine the first deal and partners (when four play). Highest cut becomes the dealer, and high cuts play as partners against low cuts. After the shuffle and cut, the dealer gives six cards to each player, three at a time, in rotation from left to right. After completing the deal, the dealer faces, or turns up, the next card to show the "trump" suit, any card of which will win over any card of another suit. If the card turned up is a jack, the dealer scores 1 point. If more than two persons are playing, only the dealer and first player can look at their hands until the turned-up card is accepted or rejected as trump. The deal passes to the left at the end of each hand.

Ranking of Cards in Seven Up

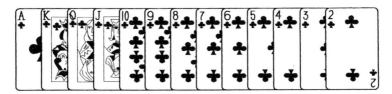

12

The Goals

The goals of the game are: (a) to hold the highest and lowest trumps in play; (b) to turn the jack for trumps or to capture it in play; and (c) to capture cards in play that count towards game.

Making the Trump

The player seated to the dealer's left has the first right to *stand* or *beg*. If she is satisfied with the trump turned, she "stands" and leads (plays the first card) to the first *trick* (sequence of cards played). If she *begs*, the dealer must either say "Take it" and give her a 1-point *gift* to let the trump stand, or deal three new cards to each player and turn up a new trump. The dealer, however, cannot give her the 1-point gift if it will give her "game" (winning) point. If the dealer chooses to give each player three more cards and turns up a trump that is the same as the first one, the dealer then repeats the process until she turns up a card of a different suit. This process is called *running the deck*. If she turns up the jack of the rejected trump suit while running the deck, she does not score 1 point for doing so. If a new trump is turned up while running the deck, all players keep their best six cards, discarding the others. However, if the dealer runs the whole deck without turning up a different trump, she collects the cards and redeals.

The Play

The player seated to the dealer's left leads any card. If the card is a trump, the players must follow suit, if possible. If the card is not a trump, the players must follow suit, but, if unable to do so, they may either play a trump or discard. The highest card in the suit led wins, unless the trick is "trumped," in which case the highest trump wins. The winner of each trick leads to the next trick.

Scoring

The players score points as follow:

> *High*—the highest trump in play. Player to whom dealt gets 1 point.
>
> *Low*—the lowest trump in play. Player to whom dealt gets 1 point.

Jack—jack of trumps. If in play, scored by the dealer turning it up as trump or by the player taking it in a trick: 1 point.

Game—won by person holding cards with the highest point count taken during play: 1 point.

In counting points for game, 10s count as 10 points; aces, 4; kings, 3; queens, 2; jacks, 1. If there is a tie for "game" between the dealer and a nondealer, the latter wins; otherwise, no one scores game point. If a player holds the only trump in play, she will win high and low, and, if the card she holds is the trump jack, she will win high, low, and jack.

Game

The player taking the greatest number of points in one hand wins the game. Many Seven-Up enthusiasts, however, prefer playing successive hands, usually two to three, until one of the players scores 7 or 10 points, as agreed to at the beginning of the game. In the latter procedure, the first player to score 7 (or 10) points wins the game. For example, if the dealer needs 1 point to "go out" and she turns the jack of trumps, she wins. If both players take enough points to win the game in the same hand, they score their points in this order: high, low, jack, and game.

Remedies and Penalties

If a player intentionally or unintentionally exposes a card, she places it face up on the table and plays it when it is legal to do so. If all players agree, they may allow the offender to keep the card in her hand during the play.

A player who revokes, or fails to follow suit when she could have done so, incurs penalties if she does not correct the revoke before the trick is *quitted* (placed face down) and the next lead made. If she does not correct the revoke, she cannot "go out" in that hand, nor can she cumulatively score more than 6 points. Additionally, if the trump jack is not in play, she forfeits 1 point of her score; if the trump jack is in play, she forfeits 2 points.

Many players prefer a stiffer penalty for a revoke, such as forfeiture of the game.

Variation

If a player begs in a three-hand game and the dealer decides to give her 1 point instead of running the deck, she must also give 1 point to the other nondealer. If the first player in a three-hand game *stands*, the next player has the right to stand or beg. If both stand, the first player leads to the first trick.

Auction Pitch, or Setback _____

Auction Pitch is basically the same game as Seven-Up with the following exceptions:

1. Two to seven players usually play *cutthroat*—each for himself. Partnership play is optional.

2. After dealing six cards to each person, three at a time, the trump suit is not decided by the dealer turning it up: instead, the players bid to name the trump suit.

3. The player seated to the left of the dealer opens the bidding. He may pass or bid from 1 to 4 points. If he bids 4 points, which is the maximum bid, he *pitches*, or leads, his trump suit immediately. If he bids less than 4 points, each player in rotation to the left may pass or bid at least 1 point more than the previous bid until a 4-point bid is made or until each player has had one opportunity to bid. Each player bases his bid on the number of points (high, low, jack, and game) he thinks he can take in play. The high bidder opens the play by pitching the trump of his choice. If he accidentally pitches the wrong card, the card pitched remains the trump card. If any player, intentionally or unintentionally, pitches a card during the bidding process, he assumes the burden of a 4-point bid.

4. If the high bidder makes his bid, he wins the hand and the game. However, as discussed above in Seven-Up, many players prefer playing until one of them scores 7 or 10 points, as agreed to at the beginning of the game. In this instance, the first person to score 7 (or 10) points wins the game, unless, of course, the pitcher (high bidder) also goes out in the same hand. In the latter case, the pitcher wins.

5. If, in playing the 7- or 10-point game, a pitcher fails to make his bid, he is set back the amount of his bid, and he subtracts that amount from his score. If he is set back more points than he has, he is said to be *in the hole*, and his score is circled or preceded by a minus sign.

6. If a player other than the pitcher revokes, the pitcher cannot be set back, and each nonoffending player scores what he makes. The revoking player, however, is set back the amount of the bid. If the pitcher revokes, he cannot score any points; instead, he is set back the amount of his bid, and the other players score what they make.

Other than the above differences, Auction Pitch and Seven-Up are the same game.

Variations
Many players like to include the jick (same color jack as trump jack) and joker in their pitch games. When they do, the jick and joker each are worth 1 point, and high cards rank as follows: ace (high), king, queen, jack, jick, joker, and 10. The jick and joker also count 1 point each in determining the winner of game point. If the players use the jick and joker, they should adjust the high bid and game score accordingly, usually 6 and 10 points, respectively.

Straight Pitch ———————————————

Straight pitch differs from Auction Pitch in the following respects:

1. After the dealer gives each player six cards, three at a time, she turns the top card of the stock to name the trump suit. There is no bidding.

2. The player sitting to the dealer's left leads to the first trick. The winner of each trick leads to the next trick.

3. The inclusion of the jick and joker in the game is common.

Ranking of Cards in Straight Pitch

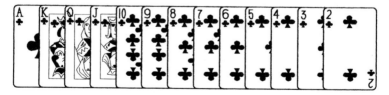

The Whist Group

Whist has its origins in the 17th-century card game of Trump. In England, Trump underwent changes to become Ruffs and Honors, which, in turn, through further refinement became Whist. In an early version, the dealer gave each player 12 cards from a 52-card deck and turned the 49th card face up as trump on the three remaining cards. The player holding the ace of trumps could "ruff," or take in the four cards and discard four cards, which could be from her hand and/or the ruff. Honors were the trump ace, king, queen, and jack.

Between the 1600s and today, card players have enjoyed many variations of Whist, including Prussian, Dummy, Double Dummy, Chinese Whist, and Norwegian Whist. The most recent innovation in Whist is Bridge and its variations.

Whist

Players and Deck Used
Whist is still a game for four players, consisting of two sets of partners, with each player holding and playing her own hand. Suits have no rank. The cards, however, rank as follows: ace (high), king, queen, jack, 10 . . . 2 (low).

Beginning the Game
The players draw cards from a deck spread face down on the table. High draws play as partners against the low draws, and the highest draw wins first deal. After the shuffle and cut, the dealer gives each player 13 cards face down and places the last card, belonging to her, face up to establish the trump suit for that deal. Before the dealer plays to the first trick, she must place the card in her hand.

The Game
The goal of the game is to take as many tricks as possible.

The Play

The person to the dealer's left makes the opening lead with a card of any suit. Each player must follow suit, if possible. Otherwise, she may play any card she chooses. Each four cards played in rotation to the left of the dealer constitutes a trick, and a trick is won by the highest card played of the suit led, or, if the trick contains a trump, by the highest trump played. The winner of a trick wins the right to make the next lead. This procedure continues until the 13th trick is quitted, or picked up and placed face down.

Scoring

The side holding the most tricks at the end of play scores 1 point for each odd trick, a trick in excess of *book* (the first 6 tricks). In addition, each side may earn points for honor cards dealt them. *Honors* are the ace, king, queen, and jack of trumps, and each is worth 1 point. If each side is dealt two honor cards, neither side counts its honors. In the longer version of the game, the first side to accumulate 7 points (or 10 points by agreement) wins the game, which will require one or, sometimes, two hands. The value of the game is the difference between the winners' and losers' scores.

Some Whist enthusiasts like playing *for a rubber,* that is, playing to win two out of three games. If the players decide to do so, they should agree on the value of a rubber (usually 2 points) at the start of the session.

Ranking of Cards in Whist

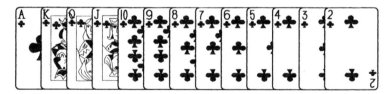

Honors for Whist

Remedies and Penalties

If a player revokes, or does not follow suit when possible, but corrects the revoke before the trick is quitted, or picked up placed face down, no penalty is incurred. Otherwise, the point won by the revoke is doubled and given to the opposing partners.

Prussian Whist

Prussian Whist differs only in the method used to determine the trump suit: Instead of the dealer's turning the last card for trump, the dealer's partner presents the deck to the player sitting at the dealer's left to cut for trump suit.

Favorite Whist

Favorite Whist differs in one respect: At the beginning of each rubber, a player cuts the deck to designate a "favorite trump." If the favorite trump reappears as trump during a game of the same rubber, tricks and honors count double.

Suit Value Whist

In Suit Value Whist, if spades are trumps, each spade trick scores 1 point; if clubs are trumps, each club trick scores 2 points; if diamonds are trumps, each diamond trick scores 3 points; if hearts are trumps, each heart trick scores 4 points. Honors have no value, and game is 10 points. The winners of the rubber earn an additional 10 points.

Dummy, or Three-Hand, Whist

In Dummy Whist, which originated in England, three players cut cards to determine possession of the dummy for successive rubbers.

(The dummy is the exposed hand played by the declarer in addition to his own hand.) Lowest cut wins the dummy for the first rubber; next lowest, for the second rubber; highest, for the third rubber. The participants must play three rubbers. The two players without the dummy play as partners against the person with the dummy. The latter faces, arranges, and plays the dummy hand after the opening lead.

Double Dummy, or Two-Hand, Whist

Two persons play Double Dummy Whist by sitting adjacent to each other so that a dummy hand is opposite each player. Otherwise, the variation chosen remains unchanged.

Contract Whist

Contract Whist differs from regular Whist in the following respects:

1. Following the shuffle, cut, and deal, and beginning with the person at the dealer's left, each player in rotation to the left bids for the right to name the trump suit. The lowest possible bid is 1 point, which requires taking 6 tricks to "make book" plus an additional 1-point trick to make the contract. The highest possible bid is 11 points, which requires taking 6 tricks to make book plus 7 tricks and all four honor cards (trump ace, king, queen, and jack) to make an 11-point contract. Honor cards are scored as in English Whist: four honors are worth 4 points; three honors are worth 2 points; one or two honors have no value.

2. The highest bidder wins the contract and leads the first trick. If possible, players must follow suit; if not possible, they may simply discard or play trump, in which case the highest trump played takes the trick. The side taking the honors in tricks scores them—not the original holders.

3. Because there is no dummy in Contract Whist, the declarer's partner plays his hand independently like other players. All other rules and scorekeeping remain the same.

The Poker Group

Poker evolved slowly from an old French game called *Gilet*, which in turn probably had its origins in the Italian game of *Primero*. During the reign of Charles IX (1560–1574), notable for its bloody civil wars between the Catholics and Huguenot Protestants, *Gilet* became the game of *Brelan*. By the time of the French Revolution, the game of *Brelan* developed into *Bouillotte*, which included such devices as the blind, freeze-out, raise, bluff, and table stakes—all of which are common to modern-day Poker.

Bouillotte also gave rise to *Ambigu*, which supplied the draw, and the English game of Brag, which was largely a bluffer's game. These three games—*Bouillotte*, *Ambigu*, and Brag—shaped modern-day Poker, along with the adoption of the 52-card deck by 1835 and the introduction of five, instead of three, dealt cards.

Basic Poker

Two to eight persons play Poker with a 52-card deck. The players sometimes limit the number of people allowed to participate according the game being played and the number of cards needed to fill out the hands. A joker may be added to the deck by mutual consent, and, if the joker is added, it is wild and is used as the holder wishes. The cards rank: ace (high) . . . 2 (low). But sometimes at the beginning of a game, the players agree to an ace's being used as high *or* low, such as in low sequences, or runs.

Seating
Players usually sit where they please, but some prefer to determine the seating arrangement by dealing each person one card face up, letting the person with low sit to the dealer's left, next low to his left, and so forth. Ties are broken by cutting for low card. The players may decide where a newcomer sits by mutual agreement, by the method above, or by some other means of choice.

Chips

By mutual consent, one player assumes the role of banker and takes charge of exchanging chips for money and for settling accounts at the end of the card session. (Matchsticks, beans, etc., may be substituted for chips.) Again by mutual consent, the players decide on the value of white, red, blue, and yellow chips.

Before the Game Begins

Poker players should decide the following at the start of the game: (a) the amount of the ante (preliminary bet made before the deal), as well as who antes (sometimes the dealer only, but usually all players); (b) a bet/raise limit; (c) a time set to stop the card session. Instead of setting a time to end a session, some players prefer playing *freeze-out*. In freeze-out, all players begin the card session with the same number of chips, and as soon as any player loses his chips, he retires from the session, which continues until one player has won all the chips. Sometimes the players also set a limit to the number of times that a bet may be raised, which oftentimes is three raises, or *bumps*.

Beginning the Game

Players customarily determine the first dealer by having the cards dealt around face up, one at a time, until a jack falls—the person who receives the first jack deals. (Some players prefer to draw or cut for high or low card to determine the first dealer.) But before the cards are actually dealt, the dealer and, sometimes, the other players, depending on the game being played, ante chips on the middle of the table to begin the "pot."

The shuffle and cut are as in other card games. However, the person sitting to the dealer's right may decline to cut the deck. If he does decline, the players to his right, in turn, may cut or decline to do so. If all players decline, the deal proceeds. The dealer gives each player his cards, one at a time, in clockwise rotation, beginning with the person to his left. (This applies to *all* Poker games.) The dealer cannot deal the last card; instead, he shuffles this card with the discards to rebuild his dealing stock.

The Stripped Deck

If there are only three or four people playing, they may choose to strip the deck of its 2s, 3s, and, sometimes, 4s. If the players strip the deck and aces are low, an 8-high straight would consist of 8, 7, 6, 5, and ace.

The Goal

The goal of each round of Poker is to hold or draw to the best hand, thereby winning the pot or a portion of it, depending on the game being played. In determining the winner(s) of each pot, the custom among poker players is to "let the cards speak for themselves."

Poker hands rank from high to low as follow:

1. **Five of a kind**. Five cards of the same rank, or denomination, which is possible only when the joker is included in the deck and/or other wild cards are named.

2. **Royal straight flush**. An ace, king, queen, jack, and 10 sequence, or run, in any suit.

3. **Straight flush**. A five-card sequence, or run, in any suit ranked by its highest card. For example, a player would call his club sequence of 10, 9, 8, 7, and 6 a straight flush, 10 high. A 10-high straight flush would rank over 9-high straight flush.

4. **Four of a kind**, which is ranked by its denomination. For example, four queens rank over four jacks.

5. **Full house**. A combination of three cards of one denomination and two cards of another: for example, three kings and two 10s. The "triplet" (three of a kind) decides rank. For example, three kings and two 10s rank over three queens and two jacks (or three kings rank over three queens).

6. **Flush**. Any five cards in a suit, but not in sequence. A player ranks a flush by the highest card in the flush.

7. **Straight**. A sequence, or run, of five cards in various suits, which is ranked by its highest card.

8. **Three of a kind**, or three cards of the same denomination, which are ranked by their denomination.

9. **Two pairs of any denominations**, which are ranked by the highest pair. For example, jacks and 5s would rank over 10s and 8s.

10. **One pair of any denomination** with three unmatched cards. A pair is ranked by denomination.

11. **High card**. A hand with none of the combinations listed above ranked by its highest card. In case of a tie, the player holding a card of the next-higher denomination wins.

Five of a Kind

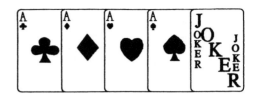

Royal Straight Flush

Straight Flush

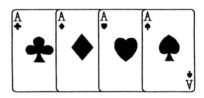

Four of a Kind

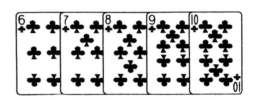

Full House

Flush

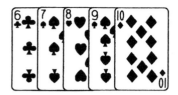 **Straight**

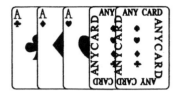 **Three of a Kind**

 **Two Pairs**

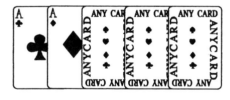 **Pair**

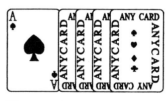 **High Card**

Ties

If the high cards in flushes tie, the next higher cards determine the winner. Ties in straight flushes, full houses, flushes, and straights divide the pot. In dividing such pots, the players usually cut for high card to determine the ownership of odd chips. If players hold four of a kind, a full house (in a seven-card game), two pairs, or one pair tie, their unmatched cards break the tie by rank. If high cards tie, the other cards again break the tie by rank.

Note: In cases where one of two tying hands has a joker, many players hold that the natural hand, the one without the joker, wins. Other players hold the opposite view, because the odds of drawing a joker are less than drawing a natural hand. But the latter group also holds that if both tying hands have multiple wild cards, the one with the fewer wild cards wins. *If a poker group wants to break ties involving wild cards by one of the methods just discussed, they should mutually agree to the method at the start of the game to avoid disputes and, perhaps, hard feelings.* Otherwise, tied hands split the pot according to guidelines set forth in the paragraph above.

Table Stakes

While a hand is in progress, a player may, with the consent of the other players, raise the betting limit to *table stakes*, which is the amount of chips he has on the table at the time. No one can raise the amount of the table stakes after looking at any of his cards. If another player does not have enough chips to *call*, or *see*, the table stakes raise, he may call a *sight* of the last bettor's cards for what chips he does have and separate that part of the pot from the rest.

The other players continue their calls and raises; some of these players also may call for a sight and thus fragment the pot further. If the person calling for a sight holds the winning hand during the showdown, he wins only that part of the pot for which he called his sight; the other players decide on the winner of the rest of the pot on the merits of their respective hands.

An accelerated variation of table stakes is the *double-up game*, wherein each player to the left of the dealer may in turn call for table stakes raises that would stop at a previously agreed-to number of such raises—usually up to six.

Remedies and Penalties

In case of a misdeal, the dealer deals again with the same pack. If a card is exposed in cutting or in reuniting a pack, the dealer must shuffle the deck again and redeal. Other misdeals include: an uncut or improperly reunited deck; a card placed face up in the deck; an incomplete or otherwise imperfect deck. If an extra but unexposed card is accidentally given to a player, the dealer can restore it to the top of the deck or continue his deal with it, whichever action is more appropriate.

If a player has a hand of fewer or more than the cards needed for the game, if he has looked at them, and if he has bet on them, his hand is foul. He then must, upon discovery, abandon the hand, forfeiting the chips he has put into the pot and even the pot itself if he won it on that deal. If a player finds that he has too many or too few cards and he has not looked at them, he may request that the dealer remedy the card count by drawing cards from his hand or by dealing additional cards to his hand to leave it at the correct number of cards. However, if more than one hand is irregular in the deal and cannot be easily remedied, the cards must be shuffled, cut, and dealt again.

If a player has looked at any of his cards, he cannot ask for a new deal unless the deck is found to be imperfect. A deal out of turn or with the wrong deck must be stopped before it is completed; otherwise, it stands.

If a player bets, calls, and/or raises out of sequence, the turn returns to the appropriate player. However, any chips the offender put in the pot remain there, and when his turn comes around, his bet, call, or raise is regarded as already made. In effect, he can make no further bets or raises until his turn comes around again, if it does. If he owes chips in addition to those put in the pot earlier, he makes up the difference. If he put too many chips in the pot, he forfeits them to the pot.

If a player announces a bet, call, or raise out of turn but does not put the chips in the pot, his announcement is void and the turn to bet, call, or raise reverts to the appropriate player.

If any player puts more chips in the pot than are required by a bet, call, or raise, he forfeits the excess chips to the pot. If he puts too few chips in the pot, he must make up the difference.

Straight, or Bluff, Poker _____

Straight Poker, the immediate forerunner of all modern-day poker games, at first required four players and a 20-card deck (aces, kings, queens, jacks, and 10s), with each person being dealt a five-card hand. Although the original game is still a popular two-hand game, it is now more often played by two to eight persons with a 52-card deck.

In Straight Poker, only the dealer antes. After she has done so and the cards are shuffled and cut, she gives each player five cards face down, one at a time, and in clockwise rotation. Beginning with the player at the dealer's left, each person, in turn, may drop from the game, check (put the lowest value of chips in the pot to remain in the game), or make a bet, placing her chips in the middle of the table. Once a bet is made, the other players remaining in the game must either call the bet or drop out of the game. A player calling a bet may also raise it, which requires the other players to call the raise if they want to stay in the game. During this round of betting and raising, a player holding a weak hand might try to bluff the others out of the game by betting and/or raising excessively, hoping thereby "to buy" the pot. If no one *sees* the bet (meets or equals it), the bettor wins the pot without having to show her cards. If the bet or bet and raises are called, all players still in the game expose their hands face up for the showdown. The best poker hand wins the pot.

Draw Poker

In Draw Poker each player antes, and the dealer gives each person five cards face down, one at a time, and in clockwise rotation. After receiving and examining his cards, each player, beginning with the one at the dealer's left, drops from the game, bets, or checks the bet of the person at his left. After all players pass or after all bets and raises have been called, each player discards his unwanted cards face down, and the dealer gives him replacements.

After the players examine the cards they received on the draw, a second round of betting takes place. Following this second betting interval, the players lay their cards face up on the table for the showdown. The person holding the best hand wins.

Variations of Draw Poker
In the game described above, a player may open the betting without

holding a pair. However, many players prefer playing a variation of Draw Poker called *Jacks or Better*, or *Jackpots*. In this variation, a player must hold a pair of jacks or a hand better than jacks in order to open the betting. In this variation, if no one can open the betting, everyone antes another chip to the pot and the cards are gathered up, shuffled, cut, and dealt again. If a person opens the betting and is later discovered to not have held the requisite cards to open, he must pay a penalty, which usually is double the size of the final pot.

Another variation of Draw Poker is *Progressive Draw Poker*, wherein a player needs jacks or better to open the betting. If no one can open with jacks or better, everyone antes another chip to the pot while the cards are gathered up, shuffled, cut, and dealt again. On the second deal, a player must have queens or better to open the betting—hence the title Progressive Draw Poker. If no one can open with queens or better, the third deal requires kings or better; the fourth deal requires aces or better; the fifth deal returns to jacks or better; and so forth. Players like this variation because it builds large pots quickly.

Another popular variation is *Pass and Out*. In this variation, a player may open the betting holding nothing more than a pair, but in each turn he must either bet or drop out. He cannot "pass," or check, the betting to the next player.

Draw Poker with a Joker

While playing Draw Poker, as well as some other games, some players like to include the joker, or *bug*, in the deck. The joker affects the game as follow:

1. The person holding the joker may use it as any card she wishes with one exception: She cannot use the joker in a flush to replace a card she already holds. For example, she cannot use it as an ace with an ace-high flush and call that flush a double-ace-high flush or straight flush. Nonetheless, the joker makes it possible for a player to hold as many as five of a kind, which ranks over all other hands.

2. For showdown purposes, if two hands are equal in all respects, the tied hands split the pot, unless the players agree at the start of the game that a natural hand ranks over one with a joker or other wild cards.

Deuces Wild

Deuces (twos) Wild is another variation of Draw Poker with a Joker. Deuces affect the game as follow:

1. Each deuce, or 2, ranks as a joker and may be used as any card its holder wishes, except the duplicate of a card he already holds in a flush, as explained in Poker with a Joker. The players also may wish to include the joker in a Deuces Wild game.

2. For showdown purposes, tied hands split the pot, unless the players agree at the start of the game that the hand with no or the fewest wild cards breaks such ties.

Wild Widow

Wild Widow is a variation of Draw Poker. The two games differ as follow:

1. The dealer gives the players four cards one at a time face down, turns the next card face up as the Wild Widow in the middle of the table, and then deals one more card face down to each person.

2. If a player holds a card or cards that match the face-up Wild Widow (the designated wild card), she may call and use them in any way she chooses, as in Deuces Wild. The players also may include the joker in the deck.

Spit in the Ocean

Spit in the Ocean is another variation of Draw Poker. The two games differ as follow:

1. The dealer gives each player four cards face down and then turns the next card, which is wild, face up in the middle of the table.

2. If a player holds a card or cards that match the face-up card, he may call and use them in any way he chooses, as in Deuces Wild.

3. Each player regards the face-up card as the fifth card of his hand, and he bases his draw on four cards only.

Lowball

Lowball is a variation of Draw Poker, in which the lowest-ranking hand, rather than the highest-ranking, wins the pot. There are no minimum requirements to open the pot, and straights and flushes do not count. In Lowball, aces are always low; hence, a pair of aces ranks lower than a pair of deuces, and the lowest hand possible is a 5, 4, 3, 2, and ace, whether it is made up of one or two suits.

During play, a player may check, or pass. If no one bets and the dealer has called for bets twice, a showdown takes place and the lowest hand wins the ante.

Ranking of Cards in Lowball

Lowest Hand of Any Suit or Combination of Suits

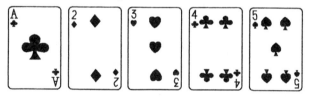

Five Card Stud

Typically, there is no ante in a Stud game, unless one has been agreed to by the players; however, if one player antes, all ante. After the shuffle and cut, the dealer gives each person one card face down (the hole card) and then one card face up, in clockwise rotation. In Five- and Seven-Card Stud, the dealer customarily announces the first bettor in each betting interval by pointing out the high card or best face-up hand. The dealer likewise points out possible hands, such as possible straights, flushes, and so forth.

The players examine their face-down cards, and the person receiving the highest face-up card must open the betting or drop from the game. In case of a tie for high card, the person receiving the first high card bets. If this person drops from the game, the person with the next highest card bets, and a betting interval follows.

After the first round of betting is completed, the dealer then gives each player still in the game a second face-up card. With two cards placed face up, the highest exposed poker combination bets first or drops from the game, as above. Thus, an ace, king outranks a queen, jack, and a pair outranks high cards. After the second round of betting, the dealer gives each active player a third face-up card, which is followed by the person with the best exposed hand opening the betting interval. Finally, the dealer gives each active player a fourth face-up card, for a total of five cards, and again the player with the best exposed hand initiates the betting interval, which is followed by the showdown. The player with the best hand wins the pot.

Remedies and Penalties

If the dealer accidentally exposes a card before a betting interval is completed, she buries that card and gives the top card to the player who would have received it if the other card had not been exposed. She completes that round of dealing with the person whose card was accidently exposed and buried.

Mexican Stud ⎯⎯⎯⎯⎯⎯⎯⎯⎯⎯⎯⎯⎯

Mexican Stud is a variation of Five-Card Stud. The two games differ as follows:

1. The dealer deals all five cards face down.

2. On receiving her second, third, fourth, and fifth cards, each player may decide which of her face-down cards to turn face up. Each player must turn a card face up before each round of betting.

Seven-Card Stud ⎯⎯⎯⎯⎯⎯⎯⎯⎯⎯⎯

As in Five-Card Stud, the ante is optional. The dealer begins the game by giving the players two cards face down and a third card face up, one at a time, which is followed by a betting interval as described in Five-Card Stud above. The dealer then gives each player her fourth, fifth, and sixth cards face up in three rounds of dealing. After each such round of the deal, the players hold a betting interval. Finally, the dealer gives each person her seventh, and last, card face down, which is followed by a final round of betting and the showdown.

In the showdown, each player selects her best five cards as her poker hand. Only in the case of tied hands would the players use their other two cards; in this event, the higher card(s) would break the tie.

Other than the number of cards and betting intervals, Five- and Seven-Card Stud are the same game.

Baseball

Baseball is the same game as Five- and Seven-Card Stud with the following exceptions:

1. All 9s, whether face up or down, and 3s face down ("in the hole") are wild.

2. If a player receives a face-up 3, he must either "buy the pot" (double its value) or drop out of the game. If he buys the pot, thus staying in the game, all 3s are wild whether face up or down (in the hole).

3. If a player receives a face-up 4, he receives another face-up card immediately as a bonus card. A 4 dealt face down (in the hole) does not earn a bonus card.

As in other Stud games, the player chooses his best five cards as his Poker hand in the showdown.

High-Low Poker

The concept of High-Low can be applied to most Poker games. When High-Low is applied, the holder of the high hand and the holder of the low hand split the pot. The holder of the high hand always wins the odd chip.

The lowest-ranking hand is called "the runt hand," and it consists of a hand of different suits whose value is less than a pair. Thus, the lowest runt possible is a 2, 3, 4, 5, and 7 of mixed suits. The highest card determines the rank of a runt.

The Showdown Games Group

Black Jack (Twenty-One) ───────────

Number of Players and Deck Used

Any number of persons may play this game (four to eight being best) with a 52-card deck and chips. The cards rank as follow: Each ace counts as either 1 or 11, depending only on the player's need; each king, queen, jack, or 10 counts as 10; each 9 . . . 2 counts as its pip, or index, value.

Chips and Bet

Before the game actually gets under way, the players agree what number of chips constitutes a minimum and maximum wager, or bet. Each player, except the dealer, must place her bet on the table in front of herself before she receives any cards at the beginning of each round of play. The dealer does not need to make a bet, because she is playing against each of the other players for whatever their individual bets may be.

Beginning the Game

In home games, the players draw or cut cards for first deal. High cut wins. The dealer shuffles, and any player may cut. The dealer then *burns* a card, that is, she turns a card from the top of the deck, makes it visible to all players, and turns it face up on the bottom of the deck, if it is not an ace. If the card is an ace, the shuffle, cut, and burn procedure is repeated. Some players will allow the dealer to slip the ace into the deck and to face and burn another card without repeating the entire shuffle, cut, and burn procedure. Then, in rotation from left to right, the dealer gives each player, including herself, one card face down, and then she deals each player, except herself, a second card face down. She deals her second card face up.

The Goal

The goal of the game is the same for all players: to hold cards whose combined pip value is 21 or the nearest possible number below 21 without exceeding 21. (Pips are the markings on the card that indicate the numerical value of the card. A 10, which has 10 pips, has a numerical value of ten.)

"Taking Hits" and Settling Wagers

If the dealer has dealt herself an ace and any other card with a pip value of 10, she announces "Black Jack" or "Twenty-One" and collects the wagers of the other players. By agreement before the game starts, the dealer may collect double the original bet. If the dealer does not announce Black Jack, each player looks at her face-down cards and mentally calculates their pip value. If any player holds a Black Jack, she announces it and collects double her bet from the dealer.

After the Black Jacks, if any, have been announced and settlements made, each player in turn, beginning with the one at the dealer's left, looks at the dealer's face-up card to help her decide whether or not she will *stand pat* or *take a hit* and thereby run the risk of going *bust*, or having cards whose count exceeds 21 points. If she is satisfied with her cards, she will say, "I'll stand pat," thereby letting the dealer know that she does not want any more cards. If she is not satisfied with her cards, she will say, "Hit me," thereby letting the dealer know that she wants one more card. If she wants more than one hit, she will say, "Hit me, again" for each additional card she wants until she is satisfied or goes bust.

Most players will ask for a hit if the pip value of their cards is 16 or less. If the pip value of their cards is 17, most players will stand pat, unless they have cause to believe that the dealer's cards have a larger combined pip value. One such cause might be that the dealer's face-up card is an 8, 9, 10, or ace. At this point, most players assess the dealer's demeanor and follow their intuition.

If the player asks for a hit and the total pip value of her cards exceeds 21, she admits that fact and forfeits her bet to the dealer. However, if the total pip value of her cards does not exceed 21 and she does not want to chance another hit, she will stand pat. Thus, each player in rotation will decide to stand pat or take a hit.

When the time comes for the dealer to make a decision to stand pat or take a hit, she turns up her hole, or face-down, card to view. The face-up cards of her opponents and her intuition will prompt her to stand pat or take a hit. Most dealers will stand pat on 17, unless their intuition prompts otherwise. (Some players make it a rule that the dealer must stand pat on 17 and collect or pay accordingly.) If the dealer overdraws or exceeds 21, she pays all players. who have not overdrawn their bets. If she stands pat, she pays all players their wagers if the pip value of their cards is greater than the pip value of her cards. She does not pay players holding cards with the same or less pip value than the cards she holds. (All ties are won by the dealer.)

In addition to the procedures above for standing pat, taking hits, and settling bets, the following variation of play may occur: If the dealer deals a player two aces or another pair whose pip value is 10 each, the player may *split the pair*, advance a second bet equal to the first, and play the aces or other pair as two separate hands. The dealer then deals a card face down to each card of the pair. When a player splits a pair, she must stand pat, take a hit, or otherwise play out the first hand of the pair before playing the second hand.

After the first round of play is completed, the dealer deals the next round from the unused stock. When the entire stock is exhausted, the dealer gathers all discards and repeats the shuffle, cut, and burn procedure given above. The deal customarily passes to a player who has Black Jack when the dealer has not done so at the same time. When this happens, the dealer completes the play for that hand before passing the deck and deal to the new dealer.

Remedies
If it is discovered that the dealer failed to burn a card, she must on demand shuffle the remainder of the deck and do so. A misdealt card can be accepted or rejected by its recipient.

Variations
While the version of Black Jack above is probably the one played most often, there are other versions with slight variations. One such variation is that the dealer gives each player, including herself, one card face down and the second card face up.

A good rule to follow is to make sure that all players understand which version and variations will be in force before starting a game. This is especially important if you are playing in professional gambling casinos like those found in states with legalized gambling.

Spanish Monte _____

Spanish Monte, a Latin American gambling game, requires a deck of 40 cards (a 52-card deck stripped of its 8s, 9s, and 10s). Any number of players may participate.

Beginning the Game

The players draw or cut for low card to determine the first dealer-banker. Ace is lowest. After the shuffle and cut, the dealer, holding the deck face down, draws two cards from the bottom of the deck and turns them face up on the table as the bottom layout. Next, he draws two cards from the top of the deck and turns them face up on the table as the top layout. After the dealer forms these two layouts, each player places his bet(s) on one or both layouts.

The Play and Settling Up

After all bets are made, the dealer turns the deck face up to expose the bottom card, which is the *port*, or *gate*, card. If the suit of the port card matches the suit of either card in the top layout, the dealer pays all bets on that layout. The same holds true if the suit of the port card matches the suit of either card in the bottom layout. If the suit of the port card does not match the suits in either the top or bottom layout, the dealer collects all bets made. Thus, the dealer pays for matches in either or both layouts and collects for no matches.

After the dealer and players settle all bets, the former turns the deck face down and gathers up and discards the four layout cards along with the port card. The dealer then forms two new layouts, as above, and again turns the deck face up to expose a new port card. Thus, the game proceeds until the deck is exhausted.

The Euchre Group

The Euchre group of card games has been closely associated with four different countries. In the United States, the game played is Euchre; in Ireland, Spoil Five; in England, Napoleon; and in France, Écarté. Enthusiasts in each country developed their own variations of the game.

The old Spanish game of *Triumphe*, mentioned in an early sixteenth-century manuscript, probably provided the origin of Euchre. The French modified Triumphe and renamed it French Ruff. With the passage of time and more modification, this game became Écarté, which was introduced by the French into the United States in Louisiana.

An interesting observation about these games is that the king outranks the ace in both Écarté and some versions of Rams (*Ramsch*), a German descendant of Euchre. In the older games, the king always headed each suit, and the ace was the lowest card. It was only after political upheaval that the ace became the highest-ranking card.

Another theory of Euchre's origin is that the game might have resulted from an effort to play the Irish game of Spoil Five with a Piquet deck. The word *Euchre* is of unknown origin, and it means, as does the word Spoil in Spoil Five, to stop or trick the maker of the trump from taking 3 tricks. An interesting note about this theory is that Spoil Five inherited its highest trump card, the trump 5, from the Irish game of Five Fingers, which, in turn, has its origins in an even older Irish card game called Maw, which was popular during the early 17th century. Since the Piquet deck had no 5, it is believed that the players used the second-ranking trump, the jack, to head the trump suit, which is, of course, characteristic of Euchre.

Euchre

Euchre is a game for four persons (two against two as partners), three persons, or two persons, the last two being played as cutthroat. The game requires a deck of 32 cards (ace, king, queen, jack, 10, 9, 8, 7), or 28 cards (ace through 8), or 24 cards (ace through 9). The joker is sometimes optionally used.

Cards rank as follow: *in trump suit*—the right bower (jack of trumps), the left bower (jack of same color), and then trump ace, king, queen, 10, 9, 8, and 7; *in suit of same color*—ace, king, queen, 10, 9, 8, 7; *in suits of opposite color*—ace, king, queen, jack, 10, 9, 8, and 7. If the joker is used, it is the highest-ranking trump, outranking both bowers.

Beginning the Game

In the draw for deal, with ace being low, low draws play as partners against the high draws. If the joker is drawn, the player must draw again. After the shuffle and cut, the dealer gives each player five cards (either three and two or two and three), in rotation to the left. The dealer turns the next card face up to propose the trump suit. After each hand, the deal passes to the left.

The dealer must redeal if the deck is imperfect, if there is a card face up in the deck, if she gives the wrong number of cards to any player, if she turns more than one card for trump, or if she does not

Rank of Cards in Play in Euchre

If Hearts Are Trump

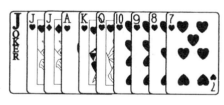

If Hearts Are Trump, Suit of Same Color

If Hearts Are Trump, Suits of Opposite Color

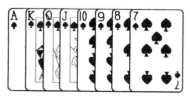

deal the same number of cards to each player in the same round.

If the joker is turned for trump, the dealer may, before looking at her hand, declare the suit that the joker represents to be trump. The players, however, may select such a suit for trump before the game or hand gets under way.

Making the Trump

The player to the dealer's left may say, "I order it up," meaning that she accepts the card turned and thus proposed as trump by the dealer, or she may pass. If the trump is ordered up, the dealer must immediately discard a card face down from her hand, though she does not take the trump card into her hand before it is her turn to play to the first trick.

If the player to the left of the dealer passes, the dealer's partner may order up the trump by saying, "I assist," or she may pass. If she passes, the next player in rotation has the same option. If all three pass, the dealer may take up the trump or pass. If the dealer passes, she puts face down the card turned as trump. If all four pass, each player in rotation to the left has one chance to name a suit trump, but not the one just rejected, or again pass. The first suit named becomes trump. If all four players pass a second time, the deal is void and passes to the left.

After the trump is taken up, any player may ask the trump maker to name the trump suit, but no one can demand to know its denomination. If the trump is the same color as the face-down proposed trump, this is called *making it next*; if it is the other color, it is called *crossing the suit*.

The person who orders up, takes up, or names the trump may play alone against both opponents. In this case, her partner lays her cards face down on the table and takes no part in the play, but she does share in her partner's victory or defeat. One partner cannot object to the other's going it alone, but the latter must announce her decision to do so when she declares the trump suit. Formerly, a dealer whose partner had assisted was allowed to go it alone; this practice is still observed in some localities.

The Goal

The goal of the trump maker and her partner is to take at least 3 of a possible 5 tricks. The goal of the opponents is to *euchre*, or stop, the trump maker from taking 3 tricks.

The Play

The person to the dealer's left or to the left of the player "going it alone," whatever the case might be, leads any card, and each player in succession plays a card in the same suit, if possible. If not possible, she must either play a trump or discard. It is not necessary to take the trick. If the trick is trumped, the highest trump wins. The winner of each trick leads to the next trick. The winner of each trick must gather it up and quit it, that is, turn it face down. Once quitted, no player may examine the trick until the end of the hand. After 5 tricks have been quitted and tallied for score, the deal passes to the left.

Scoring

If the trump maker and her partner take 3 tricks, they win the hand and the game. If they do not take 3 tricks, they are euchred and they lose the game.

Many Euchre enthusiasts prefer playing a longer game to a score of 5, 7, or 10 points, as agreed to at the beginning of the session. In these games, if the trump maker and her partner take 3 or 4 out of 5 tricks, they score 1 point towards game. If they win all 5 tricks for a *march*, they score 2 points. If the trump maker "goes it alone," she gets 4 points for a march. If the trump maker and her partner fail to get 3 tricks, they are euchred and their opponents score 2 points. Euchre players can use a long-game-scoring procedure with the one-hand, ten-minute game for wagering purposes. In the latter procedure, a scorekeeper keeps a cumulative score until the game ends.

Remedies and Penalties

If a person mistakenly "orders up" or "assists," her side must accept the burden of declaration. If a player names for trump the suit of the rejected proposed trump, her side may not make the trump for that deal.

If a player leads out of turn and everyone plays to the lead, that lead is regarded as valid, and the game continues. However, if the mistake is caught before everyone plays to the erroneous lead, any player may demand that the lead be retracted, left face up on the table, and played at the first legal opportunity. The persons who played to the erroneous lead may restore their cards to their hands without penalty. The opponent who will play last in the next lead of the offending side has the right to name the suit to be led.

If a revoke is made but caught before the trick is quitted, the player may substitute a card. However, if the revoke is not caught until after the trick is quitted, or if the offender or her partner accidentally or purposely mixes the cards, the players abandon their hands, and the nonoffenders score 2 points. If the revoke is made against a lone hand, the lone player scores 4 points.

Laps _____

In this variation of Euchre, partners playing the ten-minute game may use any points scored beyond those needed to win a game for wagering purposes. In the 5-, 7-, or 10-point game, each side may carry over to the next game any points scored beyond those needed to win a game.

Slams _____

Slams is another variation of Euchre. In the ten-minute game, if the trump maker plays a lone hand and takes 5 tricks for a march, she is credited with winning two games. In the 5-, 7-, or 10-minute game, the side that scores 5 points before the opposition can score is credited with winning two games.

Jambone _____

Jambone, a lone-hand variation, requires the lone hand to lay her cards down face up on the table and to play them. The player to her left may "call up," or name, the first card to be led by the lone player. (Among some Jambone enthusiasts, the players may take turns calling out all the cards from the Jambone hand.) If the Jambone hand wins 5 tricks in the ten-minute game, she is credited with winning two games and scores 8 points for wagering purposes. If not, regular Euchre scoring proceeds.

Jamboree

This variation of Euchre awards 16 points to the maker of the trump if she holds the five highest trumps. She automatically wins the game without having to play a card. The dealer can get credit for a Jamboree by using the turned-up, or proposed, trump card, if needed.

Cutthroat, or Three-Hand, Euchre

When three persons play, two persons play in temporary partnership against the maker of the trump. Scoring is the same as in basic Euchre, but if the temporary partners euchre the maker of the trump, they each score 2 points.

Two-Hand Euchre

When two persons play, they strip the 7s and 8s from the deck. All rules applying to the basic four-hand game of Euchre apply to its two-hand variation.

Six-Hand Euchre

When six persons participate, three play against three, and the partners sit alternately around the table. If a lone hand prevails against three opponents, he scores game. Otherwise, scoring remains the same.

Railroad Euchre ⎯⎯⎯⎯⎯⎯⎯⎯⎯⎯⎯

Railroad Euchre, a four-hand variation, differs from the basic game of Euchre as follows:

1. The players use the joker, which ranks above the right bower. They also mutually select a trump suit in advance in case the joker is turned up as the proposed trump.

2. The player going it alone may, optionally, discard one card and call for her partner's best card. The partner responds and then lays her hand face down on the table during the play. Conversely, if the dealer's partner decides to go it alone, the dealer may give her partner a card from her hand or the turned-up trump, whichever she deems better.

3. Either opponent may also call for her partner's best card to go it alone against the first lone hand. Euchre of a lone hand by two opponents scores 2 points; euchre of one lone hand by another lone hand scores 4 points. Otherwise, the scoring remains the same.

4. Euchre enthusiasts often combine Laps, Slams, Jambone, and/or Jamboree with Railroad Euchre to form variations in the game.

Buck Euchre ⎯⎯⎯⎯⎯⎯⎯⎯⎯⎯⎯

Buck Euchre requires four players to use a 24-card deck, plus the joker; five players, a 28-card deck, plus the joker; six players, a 32-card deck, plus the joker. Apart from these basic requirements, Buck Euchre differs from regular Euchre as follows:

1. Each person plays by and for himself in cutthroat fashion.

2. Before the deal, each player puts 1 chip in the pool, as agreed to at the start of the game.

3. The person ordering up or otherwise making the trump must take 3 tricks or put 1 chip in the pool for each trick he fails to take. Each trick taken is worth 1 chip. If a player takes all 5 tricks, he wins the entire pool.

Call-Ace Euchre ────────────────

The rules governing the number of players, the kind of deck used, and the deal are the same in Call-Ace Euchre as in Buck Euchre. The differences between the two games are as follow:

1. The joker is not used.

2. The dealer turns up the trump, leaving three unknown cards in the four-hand game, two in the five-hand game, and one in the six-hand game.

3. The player who orders up or names the trump may call out the best card of any suit, except trumps, and the holder of that card becomes her partner. The partner, however, remains unknown until she plays the card called out. Since all cards are not in play, the best card might be a king, queen, or jack. It might be that the trump caller is holding that card herself, in which case she would not have a partner. The trump caller also might say, "Alone," or call on a suit of which she holds the ace.

4. If the trump caller and her partner take 3 tricks, they win the hand and the game in a ten-minute game.

If the 5-, 7-, or 10-point game is being played, they each score 1 point; for a march, or 5 tricks, they each score 3 points. If they are euchred, each opponent scores 2 points. A lone hand scores 1 point for 3 tricks. For a march, the lone player scores 1 point for each person playing, including herself, in the game.

Rams (Ramsch) ────────────────

Three to five persons usually play Rams in cutthroat fashion. However, six may play, but in order to accommodate the sixth player, the dealer deals no cards to the player at her right. The game requires a 32-card deck (ace, king . . . 7 in each suit). The cards usually rank: king (high), queen, jack, ace, 10, 9, 8, and 7 (low). But, if someone declares a "General Rams," they rank: ace (high), king, queen, jack, 10, 9, 8, and 7 (low).

Ranking of Cards in General Play

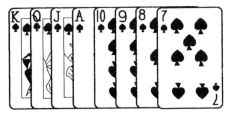

Ranking of Cards in General Rams

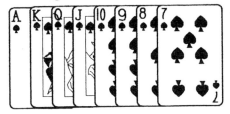

Beginning the Game

Any player deals each person one card at a time, face up, in rotation to the left, and the first person to receive a jack becomes the dealer. The dealer antes 5 chips into the pool. Then any player shuffles the cards, the dealer being last choice, and the person to the dealer's right cuts. Beginning with the player to his left, the dealer gives five cards to each person, and a *widow*, which he places face down between himself and the person to his immediate right. He deals the cards in packets of three and two or two and three, and after all hands and the widow are dealt, he turns the next card face up for trumps.

The Play

If the only chips in the pool are the dealer's ante, the pool is a *simple pool* and everyone must play. In this event, the player to the dealer's left may play with the hand dealt him, or he may discard this hand face down on the table and take up the widow. Each player, in turn, has the same options so long as no one has taken up the widow. Once the widow has been taken up, the other players must play, and the person to the dealer's left leads to the first trick.

If there are other chips besides the dealer's in the pool, the pool is a *double pool*, and the players have more options than in a simple pool. In this event, the player to the dealer's left may play with the hand dealt him, or he may discard it face down on the table and take up the widow, or he may pass. Each player, in turn, has the same options until someone takes up the widow. Once this happens, the succeeding players may either declare to play or pass. The players who have passed must not discard their hands until everyone has either declared to play or passed. No one may examine a discarded hand.

If everyone has passed except the player to the dealer's right, he must play with the dealer, and the dealer must play with him or any other player who declared to play. But if two or more declare to play, the dealer may play or pass as he chooses. The dealer may discard one card and replace it with the turned-up trump.

If any player declares a General Rams, he takes the lead and must win all 5 tricks. Each player must play in a General Rams, even if he has already passed.

Except in the case of a General Rams, the first active player to the dealer's left leads a card in any suit. Each player, in turn, must not only follow suit but must play a higher card than the one led, if possible. If not possible, he must play a trump, or a trump of greater value if a trump has been played. Even if he cannot play a trump of greater value, he must play a trump, if possible. If he can neither follow suit nor trump, he may then discard. The highest card played in the suit led wins the trick, unless someone trumps the trick, in which case the highest trump wins. The winner of the first trick leads to the second trick and so forth to the end of the hand.

Scoring
All players begin the game with the same number of chips, but only the dealer puts 5 chips into the pool. Any player who does not pass and who fails to take a trick puts 5 chips into the pool. At the end of a hand, a player takes one-fifth of the pool for each trick he takes.

If a player declaring General Rams takes all 5 tricks, he takes the pool, and each player gives him an additional 5 chips. If he fails, he must give each player 5 chips and double the pool.

Remedies and Penalties
The rules of Euchre apply.

Bierspiel ————————————————

Bierspiel, another variation of Rams, requires a 32-card deck. Bierspiel and Rams differ as follow:

1. The cards rank as in Rams, except that the diamond 7 always ranks as the second-highest trump, regardless of what suit is trump. Thus the ranking is: king (high), diamond 7, queen, jack, ace, 10, 9, 8, and 7 (low). If the dealer turns the diamond 7 as trump, he must turn up the next card for trump. If he declares to play, he may take both cards into his hand, discarding two others. If the dealer passes, the player to his left may pick up the two cards.

2. If four players declare to play, the first three leads must be trumps; if three declare, the first two leads; if two declare, the first only. If the leader has no trumps, he must put his lowest card face down on the table, and the other players having trumps must play trumps on it. If one of these players has no trumps, he, too, may play his low card face down on the pile.

3. The player taking the most tricks wins the hand, game, and stakes in the one-hand/ten-minute game.

Originally, Bierspiel, like Dominos, was a popular beer hall game and was scored similarly. Thus, each player begins the game with three crosses chalked before him, each worth 5 points. If he scores 1 point, he erases the middle of the first cross, leaving it worth 4 points. He subsequently erases one arm of the cross for each point scored. The first player to erase the 3 middles of the crosses and their 12 points, for a total of 15 points, wins the game. Scoring can be done with pencil and paper.

Other than the differences noted above, Bierspiel is the same game as Rams.

Ranking of Cards in Bierspiel if Hearts are Trump

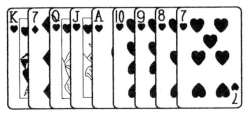

Loo, or Division Loo _____

Three to 17 players may play Loo, but the usual number ranges from five to eight. Since a pool is part of Loo, each hand, which requires about five minutes of play, is a game; play may be terminated at the end of each game. Loo requires a 52-card deck, and the cards rank: ace (high), king, queen, jack, 10 . . . 2 (low).

Ranking of Cards in Loo

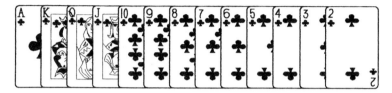

Beginning the Game

To determine the dealer, a player picks up the deck and deals cards one at a time, face up, to the players until someone receives a jack. The person receiving the jack becomes the dealer, whereupon the cards are shuffled and cut. The dealer then puts 3 chips into the pool and gives each player three cards, one at a time, in rotation from left to right. The dealer does not turn a trump when there are only 3 chips in the pool, which is a *simple pool*. This deal is known as a *bold stand* because each person must play the hand dealt her.

The Play

The player to the dealer's left may lead any card. The other players must not only follow suit, if they can, but they must try to head, or take, the trick. The cards are not gathered in as tricks but are left face up in front of each player. If everyone follows suit, the winner of the trick leads to the next trick, and so forth. If one or more players do not follow suit, the dealer turns the top card of the stock for a trump before her next lead. The winner of the prior trick must lead a trump to the next trick, if possible. If trumps fall on a trick, the highest trump wins the trick.

The players who have won tricks take one-third of the pool for each trick taken. The players who did not win tricks are "looed" and must put 3 chips into the new pool, which is now a *double pool*.

Again, the dealer puts 3 chips into the pool, deals as before, except now she deals a widow just before she deals her own hand, and then turns over a trump. Beginning with the player to the dealer's left, each player, in turn, has the choice of standing on the cards dealt her, exchanging her hand for the widow, if it has not yet been picked up, or passing. Any player standing or exchanging will be looed, unless she wins a trick. If all pass but the player to the dealer's right, she must play the hand, take the widow, or surrender the pool to the dealer.

If only one player stands and has not taken the widow, the dealer must stand or defend with the widow. If she takes any tricks, she leaves her winnings in the pool. If she is looed, she does not pay. If the one player standing has taken the widow, the pool is hers, unless the dealer will play against her on her own account.

If all players declare trump, the one to the dealer's left leads. She must lead a trump, if possible, and she must lead the highest trump of two or more in her hand. The winner of the trick must lead a trump, if possible. Each player, in turn, must follow suit and must try to take the trick. However, she need not throw down a trump on a trick that is of lower value than a trump that has fallen. The winners of the 3 tricks again divide the pool—one-third for each trick taken. The players who have been looed put 3 chips in the next pool. If no one is looed, the next pool will be a simple pool. The deal passes to the left.

The version of Loo described above is *Limited Loo*. In *Unlimited Loo*, each player led must double the amount in the current pool as the basis for the next one.

Loo with Flushes
Loo players sometimes agree to play flushes. If they do so agree, any player in a double pool holding three trumps, either dealt to her or found in the widow, waits until all the players—including the dealer—have declared or passed. She then shows her flush in trumps and takes the pool without playing for it, thereby looing the other players. If two players hold trump flushes, the one sitting closest to the dealer's left wins the pool, regardless of the rank of the cards; but the other flush is not looed.

Remedies and Penalties

If a person deals the wrong number of cards or hands, she loses the deal and pays 3 chips to the pool, making the next one a double pool. If a player revokes by failing to follow suit, to take a trick, or to lead a trump when so required, the other players holding cards divide the pool equally among themselves. The offender antes up 6 chips for the next pool.

Irish Loo

Irish Loo differs from Loo in the following respects:
1. In Irish Loo, there is no distinction between pools.
2. There is no widow.
3. The dealer always puts a trump face up on top of the stock.
4. The dealer asks those who stand if they wish to exchange any cards. If so, they discard their unwanted cards, and the dealer gives them replacement cards from the top of the stock.

Five-Card Loo

Five-Card Loo differs from Loo as follows:
1. In this version, the dealer antes 5 chips into the pool and deals five cards to each player.
2. A flush of five cards wins the pool without playing.
3. Anyone sitting at the table, whether he plays or passes, is looed if he does not take a trick. Looed players must pay 5 chips to the pool.

Napoleon, or Nap

Napoleon requires a 52-card deck and from two to six players, with four being the norm. Each person plays for himself. The cards rank: ace (high), king, queen, jack, 10, 9, 8, 7, 6, 5, 4, 3, and 2 (low). Ace is highest in play, but lowest in cutting.

Ranking of Cards in Napoleon

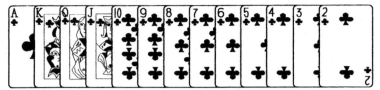

Beginning the Game

Low draw or cut determines first dealer. After the shuffle and cut, the dealer gives each player five cards in two rounds of dealing: either three and two or two and three. Both the bidding and play begin with the person at the dealer's left. A misdeal requires a new deal by the same dealer.

Bidding

Beginning at the dealer's left, each player, in turn, either may bid the number of tricks he plans to take, if allowed to name trumps, or he may pass. If he bids, he does not name his intended trump suit. Each player has only one chance to bid or pass—the dealer being last. The successful bidder then names his trump suit. Sometimes a player may bid 3 no-trump, called "misery." This bid ranks above 3 with trumps, but below 4 with trumps. Usually, a bid of 5 with trumps, called "Nap," is the highest possible bid. If no one bids, the dealer must bid at least 1 trick.

Some Nap players allow two other bids that successively outrank Nap: Wellington and Blucher. While each of these bids contracts to take 5 tricks with trumps, they differ in the scoring.

The Play

The trump maker must lead trumps to the first trick. Other leads may be in any suit. Each player must follow suit, if possible; if not possible, he must play a trump or discard. The winner of each trick leads the next, and each player must quit tricks face down in such a manner as to make them easy to count. Players may not examine quitted tricks. The highest card of the suit led wins the trick, unless it is trumped, in which case the highest trump wins. As soon as the bidder takes the tricks needed to make his bid, the players abandon the rest of the hand, paying the appropriate number of chips. At the end of each hand, the deal passes left.

Scoring

At the beginning of the game, all players start with the same number of chips. (Scores may be kept with pencil and paper.) In the ten-minute/one-hand game, if the trump maker succeeds in making his bid, each opponent pays him 1 chip for each trick bid; if he fails, he pays each opponent 1 chip for each trick bid. Misery is paid for as 3 tricks. The trump maker wins 10 chips from each player for Nap, if successful; if not, he pays only 5 chips to each player. He wins 5 chips from each player for a "Wellington," if successful; if not, he pays 10 chips to each player. He wins 10 chips from each player for a "Blucher," if successful; if not, he pays 20 to each player.

If the players want a longer game, they set a time limit. In this procedure, the player with the most chips or highest score wins the game. An alternate procedure requires play to stop as soon as one player runs out of chips.

Remedies and Penalties

A claim of misdeal arising from an incorrect number of cards must be made by a player before he bids or passes. Otherwise, he must play out the hand. If the trump maker holds the correct number of cards in the preceding case and another player does not, the latter must pay the former if he makes his bid. If the trump maker holds too many cards, he scores nothing for making his bid. If the trump maker holds too few cards, he must pay or be paid as he loses or wins. The trump maker loses any trick on which he has no card to play.

A trump maker who leads out of turn must take back the card, unless all have played to it, in which case the trick stands. An opponent who leads out of turn pays 3 chips to the trump maker and is not paid if the latter loses. If the trump maker revokes, he must pay the amount of his bid to each opponent, as each opponent must do if one of them revokes. When a revoke is discovered, the players abandon the rest of the hand.

The Cassino Group

By the 15th century, Cassino had worked its way from Italy into France, where it remained a favorite game for several hundred years. Today, some people regard Cassino as being on the same level as Fish or Old Maid, but such a view overlooks the powers of observation, memory, and inference needed to win.

Cassino

Cassino requires two or three persons playing as individuals, or four persons playing as partners, two against two, and a full deck of 52 cards. Although the cards have no ranking, they do have the following numerical value: each ace counts 1; each 2, 3, 4, 5, 6, 7, 8, 9, and 10 counts its pip, or index, value; and each jack, queen, and king counts 0, because it has no numerical value.

Beginning the Game

The players draw or cut cards to determine first deal and, if four play, partnerships. Low cut wins first deal (ace being low), and, if four play, low cuts play as partners against high cuts. If four play, partners sit facing each other.

After the shuffle and cut, the dealer gives each player four cards face down, in two rounds of two cards each. He then deals four cards face up on the table and places the remainder of the cards, or the stock, face down on the table. After all players have used their first four cards, the dealer gives each player four cards, two at a time, but none to the table. This routine continues until all cards have been dealt and played. If, during the last deal of the hand, there are not enough cards to be dealt evenly around the table, the dealer takes fewer cards than his opponent(s). The deal passes to the left.

The Goal

The goal of play is to score points by taking certain cards and card combinations having point value. The table below provides the point value of scoring cards.

	Points
Cards (greatest number taken in play):	3
Spades (greatest number taken in play):	1
Big Cassino (diamond 10):	2
Little Cassino (spade 2):	1
Each ace, counting 1, totals:	4
Sweep (taking all cards face up on table):	1

If a tie occurs in the count of spades or cards, they are not scored.

The Play

In Cassino, there are four basic taking plays. The **first** is *taking in combination*. If a player holds a card in his hand of the same rank, or denomination, as one face up on the table, he may show/play his card and take in the two cards as a trick. If several such cards are on the table, he may take them all in on the same play. For example, if he holds a 5 and there are two other 5s face up on the table, he may play his 5 and take in all three 5s in one play. Note that pairing is the only way that a player may take in jacks, queens, and kings.

A player may also take in two or more cards whose combined pip value equals the pip value of a card in his hand. For example, a player may take a 5, 3, and ace from the table if he holds a 9 in his hand. An ace always counts as 1 towards such a combination. All other cards count their pip value.

The **second** basic play is *building a combination*. A player may take a card from his hand and add it to one or more cards face up on the table if he holds in his hand another card of the pip value needed to take this combination on his next turn to play. For example, he may take a 3 from his hand, add it to a 4 face up on the table, and say, "I'm building a 7." He must, however, announce the rank of the build, such as "7s." If he fails to announce the rank, the next player may undo the build, separate the cards, and use them as he pleases. In the meantime, however, another player may take the combination or build it to a higher combination. A player may increase his own build on a succeeding turn at play only if he holds cards that would enable him to take both builds.

The **third** basic play is *calling a combination*. For example, if a player holds two or more 7s and another 7 and/or group of cards whose pip value equals 7 is on the table, he may say, "I call 7s," and add one of his 7s to the 7 and/or the group of cards, planning to take them on his next turn at play. He must clearly state that he *calls*, not *builds*; if he does not, the next player may point out the omission, separate the cards, and use them as he wishes. In the meantime, however, another player may take the combination. Unlike a build that can be built higher, a called combination cannot be altered.

A player may continue to make builds or calls, take another combination, or take another player's build or call before taking in his first build or call. If he cannot make further builds or calls or take other combinations, he may take his first build or call, or he may simply place a discard face up on the table, which is called "trailing."

The **fourth** basic play is *making a sweep*. Making a sweep occurs when a person plays a card that takes every card that is face up on the table. For example, if a player holds a 10 in his hand and if a 2, 3, 4, and ace are the only cards face up on the table, he may play his 10, announcing a sweep, and pick up the face-up 2, 3, 4, and ace. A player marks a sweep as a trick by turning face up one card on the combination.

If a player cannot make one of these basic four plays, he must place a card from his hand face up on the table. After the last deal in the hand and no further play is possible, the player taking in the last combination also takes in any cards remaining on the table. This play, however, does not score as a sweep.

Scoring

The partnership or person scoring the greatest number of points wins the hand and game.

Many Cassino enthusiasts prefer playing to 21 points, with the player taking the most points declared winner. If the players or sides have tied scores, the tie is broken by the following: (a) the majority of cards, (b) the majority of spades, (c) Big Cassino, (d) Little Cassino, (e) aces (spade, club, heart, and diamond), and (f) the majority of sweeps.

Remedies and Penalties

If the dealer misdeals during the opening deal of a game, where each hand is a game, he must give an exposed card to the table and give the intended recipient another card from the top of the stock. After the opening deal, a subsequent misdeal forfeits the game and the deck to the opponent(s).

If the dealer misdeals during the opening deal of a game, where game is 21 points, the dealer remedies the misdeal as above. However, subsequent misdeals do not forfeit the game and deck. Instead, the dealer buries the exposed card in the stock and replaces it with one from the top of the stock.

If a player finds that he has the wrong number of cards on any deal but the opening one, he must correct the error by either returning cards to or drawing cards from the stock.

If a person plays a card out of turn, he must place it face up to one side and then play it to the table on his next turn at play. Any cards taken by a play out of turn must be restored to the table.

If a player makes a build or call but does not hold the necessary taking card(s), he must separate the cards on the table, and, if his opponent(s) so choose, they may take back any cards played after the offense was committed and play other cards in their place. If another player has already taken the erroneous build or call, there is no remedy.

A player may look at the last played and quitted trick so long as he does so before he plays to the next trick. Otherwise, he will incur a penalty of 1 point for each trick examined.

Royal Cassino _____

Royal Cassino differs from Cassino as follows:

1. In Royal Casino, an ace counts as 1 or 14, as the player chooses at the time; a king counts 13; queen, 12; jack, 11; and all other cards count their pip value.

2. The player may use face cards in builds and duplicate builds.

Royal Draw Cassino

Royal Draw Cassino differs from Royal Cassino as follows:

1. Each player draws a card from the top of the stock each time he plays or discards. Thus, each player always holds four cards until the hand closes.

2. If a player fails to draw in turn, he draws two cards in his next turn at play.

3. After the stock is exhausted, play continues as in regular Cassino.

Spade Cassino

Spade Cassino differs from Cassino as follows:

1. The jack, 2, and ace of spades are each worth 2 points; each other spade counts as 1 point.

2. Game is 61 points. The players may record their scores with pencil and paper or with a cribbage board. The first player to score or peg 61 points wins, either during play or at the end of a hand.

The Hearts Group

The primary goal of Hearts and its variations is to avoid taking certain cards and tricks or, in some cases, to take them all. Such a goal provides solace for those who get low-ranking cards and no trumps on the deal, because in these games it is desirable to hold cards that will take few, if any, tricks. A similar objective led to the development of Nullo and to its introduction into various forms of Whist, Euchre, Skat, and other games. Here again poor cards are highly esteemed and taking certain tricks is disastrous. The skill needed for these games is the ability to lose both strategically and overwhelmingly.

When sitting down to play Hearts with a new group, you should review the rules of the game you are about to play, because there are variations in each Hearts game and you might find yourself playing one game while your new friends are playing another.

Hearts

Hearts requires a full deck of 52 cards and three to six players, with four players being best. The cards rank: ace (high), king, queen, jack, 10, 9 . . . 2 (low). The game has no trump suit.

Ranking of Cards in Hearts

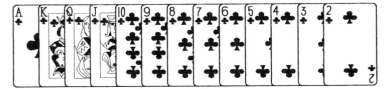

Beginning the Game
The players draw or cut cards for first deal, which is won by the lowest draw. After the shuffle and cut, the dealer gives each player, in rotation to the left, one card at a time until the entire deck is dealt.

The dealer then sets aside any odd cards left over from the deal as a widow, which is picked up by the winner of the first trick.

The Goal
The goal of the game is to take no heart tricks, as few as possible, or to take all of them and add 13 points to your opponents' scores. Low score wins the game.

The Play
Keeping the goal of the game in mind, the player at the dealer's left leads to the first trick. In rotation from left to right, each player must follow suit, if possible, or otherwise discard. In the latter case, it is good strategy to throw off a heart, especially a high one; doing so may help to avoid taking a round of hearts later. The person playing the highest card of the suit led wins the trick and leads to the next trick. After the last trick has been quitted, the players count the hearts taken and settle up accordingly before the cards are shuffled, cut, and dealt for a new game.

Scoring
Each deal is a game in itself, unless the game continues until a player reaches a predetermined score or until a specified time limit has elapsed.

If each deal is a game, the players count their hearts and pay one chip for each heart taken, and the player who takes the fewest hearts wins all the chips thus paid. (A scorekeeper can record the scores with pencil and paper, thus avoiding the use of chips, beans, matchsticks, etc.) If two or more players tie for low score, they divide the pool, leaving odd chips in the pool for the next game.

Alternative methods of scoring are to continue play until one person accumulates a certain number of points, such as 26, 39, 52, or until a specified amount of time has elapsed, either of which events marks the end of the game. With either of these methods, the person with the greater score would pay each other player the difference between their scores.

Remedies and Penalties
Any misdeal requires a new deal by the next player in turn, except

when the deck is imperfect. In the latter case, the same person deals again with a perfect deck. If some players have too few cards and other players have too many, and if no one has looked at their cards, they may by agreement adjust the cards among themselves to remedy the misdeal.

If a player leads or plays out of turn, he must withdraw the card, unless all have played to the trick, and the trick has been quitted. In the latter case, the play is valid.

If a player revokes, or fails to follow suit when he could have done so, he may correct the revoke if he does so before the trick is quitted. Otherwise, the players abandon their hands, and the revoker must put 13 chips into the pool for the next hand or add 13 points to his score. If two or more players revoke, each separately must pay the full penalty. If the revoking player has a partner, the former must pay his partner's penalty.

A player must take the last trick if, at the last round of play, he is short one card. If his hand is several cards short, he must take each trick to which he cannot play a card.

Black Jack Hearts

In this variation of Hearts, the jack of spades counts 10 points against the person taking it but ranks as a spade in play. The holder of the jack of spades must follow suit to a spade lead unless he has another spade he would rather play. Otherwise, he may discard the jack of spades as he would a heart.

Red Jack Hearts

In this variation the jack of diamonds, called "red jack," ranks as a diamond but counts as 10-plus points for the person taking it in play. In other words, the player taking the jack of diamonds can use its plus value to reduce his score by 10 points or to add 10 points to each opponent's score. The holder of the jack of diamonds must follow suit to a diamond lead unless he has another diamond to play. Other than the 10-plus points feature, players score the same as they would in regular Hearts.

Players may use the Red Jack variation in any game of Hearts.

Two-Ten-Jack _____

Two-Ten-Jack is a Hearts variation having cards with plus- and minus-counting values. The game requires a 52-card deck and two to four players, with the two-hand game usually rated best.

In Two-Ten-Jack, hearts are always trumps, but the ace of spades, called *speculation*, ranks as the highest trump. Thus, trumps rank ace of spades (high), and then the following hearts: ace, king, queen, jack, 10 . . . 2 (low). Spades rank: king (high) . . . 2 (low); diamonds and clubs rank: ace (high), king, queen, jack, 10 . . . 2 (low).

Trumps Ranking in Two-Ten-Jack

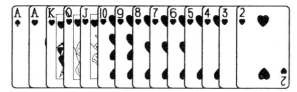

Spades Ranking in Two-Ten-Jack

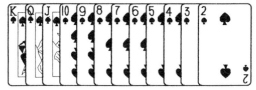

Diamonds and Clubs Ranking in Two-Ten-Jack

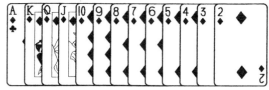

Beginning the Game

The players draw or cut cards for first deal; low draw wins. If four persons play, low cuts play as partners against the high cuts. After the shuffle and cut, the dealer gives each player six cards, one at a time face down, beginning with the person seated to his left. The dealer then places the remainder of the deck face down on the table as the stock.

The Goal

The goal of the game is to take tricks with cards of plus-counting value and to avoid tricks with cards of minus-counting value. The cards having plus- and minus-counting value appear in the table below:

		Points
Cards of Plus Value:	Heart 2, 10, Jack	10
	Heart Ace, King, Queen	5
	Diamond Ace, King, Queen, Jack	1
	Club Ace, King, Queen, Jack	1
Cards of Minus Value:	Spade 2, 10, Jack	10
	Spade Ace*, King, Queen	5

The Play

With these goals in mind, the opponent may lead any card to the first trick, and the dealer must always follow suit with one exception: If a heart is led and the dealer holds no hearts, but has the ace of spades, he is not obliged to play the latter. He may withhold it, "speculating" that he might be able to take the 2, 10, or jack of hearts in a later trick. However, if the opponent leads a spade, the dealer must play the ace of spades if he holds no other spade. The highest card of the suit led takes the trick, unless trumped, in which case the trump wins.

The winner of the first and succeeding tricks draws a card from the top of the stock, and the loser takes the next card. The winner of a trick leads to the next one. This routine continues until the stock and hands are exhausted, which marks the end of play.

Scoring

At the end of play, each person tallies his plus and minus points and then subtracts the smaller number from the larger one. If the larger score is plus, the scorekeeper records the difference as a plus number; if minus, as a minus number. The players may regard a plus 30 points or a plus 100 points as a game.

---

*Though the ace of spades has a minus value, its holder can take the 2, 10, or jack of hearts in play for a plus value of 5 points; he can take the ace, king, or queen of hearts and break even; and he can take the ace, king, queen, or jack of diamonds and lose 4, instead of 5, points.

Black Lady (Black Maria) _____

Black Lady seems to be the most popular variant of Hearts. (Black Lady refers to the queen of spades.) Black Lady is the same game as Hearts with the following exceptions:

1. The Black Lady retains her rank as a spade, but she counts 13 points against the person taking her in a trick.

2. Following the deal, each player passes three cards from her hand to the person to her left. Some players prefer to make passes alternately to the left, across the table, and then to the right. Each player must pass three cards before looking at those passed to her.

The pass gives everyone a chance to get rid of unwanted cards; consequently, each player should try to keep cards that will minimize her chances of taking the queen of spades and/or a number of heart tricks. If a player gets the queen of spades on the deal, she should keep it if she has at least three other spades to shield it from being flushed out during play, and try to sluff it off, or discard it, as quickly as possible. To make this task easier, she should try to strip her hand of clubs or diamonds while passing off cards.

3. If, on the other hand, a player is dealt a strong heart hand (for example, the ace, king, queen, and jack of hearts) and the ace, king, *or* queen of spades, she should try to *shoot the moon, take all,* or *slam,* which is another new element introduced to Hearts by the Black Lady. In order to shoot the moon, a player has to take all 13 hearts and the spade queen. If she succeeds, she will give each of her opponents 26 points; if she fails, she scores all the points she has taken in tricks.

4. Another new element introduced to Hearts by the Black Lady is that whoever holds the 2 of clubs must lead it to the first trick. If no one holds the 2 of clubs, then the holder of the club 3, 4, etc., leads.

Each player must follow suit, if possible. If not possible, the player may discard, or sluff off, an undesirable card, such as a heart or queen of spades, unless the players have agreed beforehand that there will be "no dirt" (a heart or queen of spades) played on the first trick. If such an agreement has been made, the player must discard otherwise, perhaps a high spade that she might have received on the pass. The winner of the first trick also takes the widow, if there is one. Some players avoid taking the first trick, fearing that the queen of spades might be lurking in the widow. The winner of each trick leads to the next trick.

When it becomes apparent that one player is trying to shoot the moon, the others try to stop her, even if it requires taking the queen of spades. Taking 13 points is preferable to taking 26 points.

5. Although any of the scoring procedures discussed under Hearts above may be used, most players seem to prefer playing to 100 points. The first person to reach 100 loses and ends the game simultaneously. In settling accounts, if playing for money, the high scorers pay the difference between their scores and the low score.

The second-most preferred method of scoring in Black Lady is simply to set a time limit.

The Solitaire Group

Solitaire, or Patience, includes all games that can be played by one or two persons with a single or double deck of cards, in which the goal is to take cards from the top of the shuffled deck and arrange them in some systematic order. There are many games of Solitaire for two or more players, but their inventors designed most of them to be played by one person. Consequently, the whole group of Patience games is generally known as Solitaire, which is any game that one person can play alone. Many games of Patience have become very popular gambling games.

Firing Squad

Firing Squad requires a full deck of 52 cards, which in play rank: ace (high) . . . deuce, or 2, (low). There is no *tableau*, or layout.

Beginning the Game
After shuffling and cutting the deck, turn four cards face up horizontally across the middle of the table. Subject to the rules of elimination given below, each of these four cards forms the top of a vertical column, to which you will add cards or from which you will remove cards.

The Goal
The object of the game is to strip these columns by eliminating cards until each column consists of one ace and no other card.

The Play
After laying out the first four cards, you may lay out four more and begin the eliminations across the horizontal rows if two or more cards are of the same suit or suits. To eliminate the cards, place in a discard, or trash, pile all cards of smaller denominations exposed in each suit, leaving only the higher or highest card of each suit

Foundation Row for Firing Squad

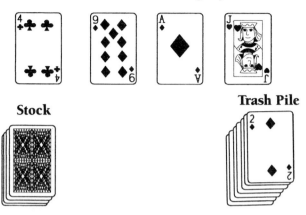

Stock

Trash Pile

exposed. If you play out four cards of different suits on the first or any subsequent horizontal row, you cannot eliminate any cards.

Next, play out one card on each of the first four cards or on those remaining, filling in column spaces where cards were eliminated. If you can later fill an empty column space with the topmost exposed card from another column (the last card played), you must do so. Doing so will allow you to uncover buried cards.

You must always play out four cards at a time until the end of the deck is reached, which marks the end of play.

Game
You win the game only if you manage to strip down each column, by elimination, to one ace.

Variations
You will find it very difficult to win this game. To increase your odds for a win or simply to lessen your frustration, you might want to try one of these alternate variations of play: (a) play through the discard pile four cards at a time; (b) turn face up and run through the deck six, instead of four, cards at a time; (c) play several games and tabulate the cards not eliminated in each game—low score, of course, would win. Similarly, you might like to play simultaneously and competitively with two or more players, with the winner being the player holding the fewest cards after having run the deck once.

Note: You may vary the play of any Solitaire game by devising a different method of constructing discard piles, by permitting new deals, or by developing other variations to make the game more interesting and playable. Moreover, you may play them in competition with two or more players, and, where foundation aces are played to, all players may play to other players' foundation aces.

Auld Lang Syne

Auld Lang Syne requires a 52-card deck. The cards rank: king (high) . . . ace (low).

Beginning the Game
Place the four aces in a horizontal foundation row and shuffle the remainder of the deck.

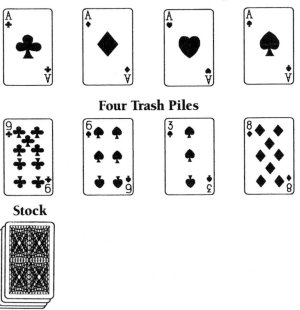

Foundation Row for Auld Lang Syne

Four Trash Piles

Stock

The Goal
The goal of the game is to build on each ace an upward, or ascending, sequence by rank only.

The Play
As you deal the cards, one at a time, on four discard, or trash, piles,

build on the foundation aces in upward, or ascending, sequence by rank only, ignoring suit and color. You may move only one card at a time from a discard pile to a foundation pile, and you are permitted only one pass through the deck.

Game
You win the game if you play all the cards on the foundation aces. Otherwise, you lose.

3s in the Corner

3s in the Corner, which utilizes an unusual *tableau* and around-the-corner sequences, requires a 52-card deck.

Beginning the Game
After shuffling and cutting the deck, lay out five cards face up to form a Greek cross, that is, a three-card horizontal row with the

Tableau for 3s in the Corner

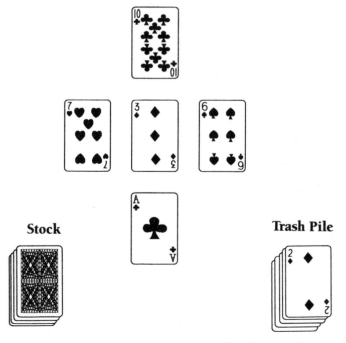

Stock   **Trash Pile**

fourth card above the middle card and the fifth card beneath the middle card. The Greek cross is the tableau, or layout, and the undealt portion of the deck is the *stock*.

The Goal

The goal of the game is to complete four upward sequences from the foundation 3s by rank and suit.

The Play

On the cards of the tableau, build downward, around-the-corner sequences by rank: only, ignoring suit and color. On the tableau, the cards rank: 2 (high), ace, king, queen, jack, 10, 9, 8, 7, 6, 5, and 4 (low). The 3s are foundation cards to be played as described below. To fill in the layout, turn cards face up from the top of the stock, one at a time, and place the playable cards directly over the tableau cards to maintain the cross structure. If you cannot play a card from the stock, turn it face up on the *discard*, or *trash, pile*. Once you have the discard pile started, you can play the topmost card of the discard pile on the tableau or foundation 3s. If such a play is made, the card beneath the card just played becomes available for play immediately. You can remove only one card at a time from the discard pile.

Whenever you get a 3, either in the layout or stock, place it as a foundation card in one of the four corners of the cross. On each of these 3s, build an upward sequence by rank and suit: for example, the 3, 4, 5, 6, 7, 8, 9, 10, jack, queen, king, ace, and deuce (2) of clubs. One by one, you will hopefully turn cards from the stock face up that can be played to the tableau or to the foundation 3s.

Game

You win the game if you complete all four upward sequences from the foundation 3s. The odds for winning are about one in three.

Good Measure _____

Good Measure requires the player, using a 52-card deck, to set up part of the foundations and all of the stock before beginning the *tableau*. The cards rank: ace (low) . . . king (high).

Beginning the Game

Strip two aces from the deck and place them in the *foundations* area. You will similarly place the other two aces as they appear in play. Next, shuffle and cut the remainder of the deck and deal out 10 five-card piles as *stock*, placing the topmost card face up on each pile.

Foundation Row for Good Measure

Stock Piles

The Goal

The goal of the game is to play all cards to the foundations in upward, or ascending, sequence (ace to king) by rank and suit.

The Play

When the other two aces appear in play, place them in the foundations row; when the kings appear, place them just above the stock but below the foundations row to form the tableau.

In play, build an upward sequence by rank and suit off of each ace. On the 10 five-card piles of stock and on the kings, build downward sequences by rank only, ignoring suit and color. Only the top card on each pile of stock is available for play. You may not fill a vacated space among the piles of stock: A space remains a space for the duration of the game.

Continue the play in this manner until the game ends.

Game

The game comes to an end either when you have played all cards to the foundations, in which case you win, or until you reach a block and can play no further, in which case you lose the game.

Note: If you want a more challenging game, build off the kings in downward sequences by rank and in alternating colors.

Klondike

Klondike, which also requires a 52-card deck, is probably the best-known and most-often-played game of Solitaire. The cards rank: ace (low) . . . king (high).

Beginning the Game

After shuffling and cutting the deck, begin your *tableau* as follows: one card turned face up with six other cards face down to form a seven-card horizontal row. Next, turn a card face up on the second card of the row and then place five cards face down, one on each of the remaining face-down cards. Repeat this procedure with five, four, three, two, and one cards. The completed tableau has 28 cards, with the piles containing respectively one, two, three, four, five, six, and seven cards, each topped with a face-up card. You will use the remaining 24 cards as *stock*.

The Goal

The goal of the game is to use all stock, discard (trash), and tableau cards to build on each foundation ace an upward, or ascending, sequence by rank and suit (aces to kings).

Foundation Row for Klondike

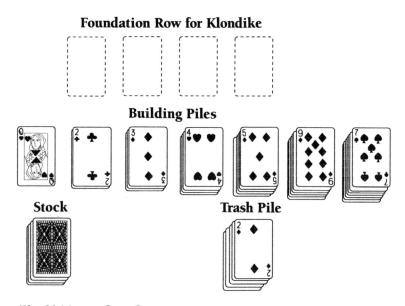

Building Piles

Stock

Trash Pile

The Play

Play any ace face up on the tableau to the foundations row above. On each foundation ace, you must build an upward, or ascending, sequence by rank and by suit. On the face-up cards in the tableau, build downward, or descending, sequences by rank and in alternate colors. You may fill spaces in the tableau only with kings face up in the stock or with kings and king-high sequences face up in the tableau. If you move one card of a sequence to another pile in the tableau, you must move the whole sequence with it. Some Klondike players follow a more liberal rule that allows them to move only part of a sequence as long as the bottom card moved is one rank lower and the opposite color of the card being played to.

After all possible tableau manipulations have been made, turn the cards in the stock face up one at a time and, if possible, play them on foundation or tableau piles. If these plays are not possible, place the card face up on the *discard*, or *trash*, *pile*. If you play a card from the discard pile, the one beneath immediately becomes playable.

After you have run through the stock once, the game ends.

Settling Up

If playing for stakes, you will have probably paid 52 chips for the deck, but will earn back 5 chips for each card played to a foundation pile.

The Masked Twelve _____

The Masked Twelve, which has an unusual *tableau*, requires a deck of 52-cards. The cards rank: ace (low) . . . king (high).

Beginning the Game

After shuffling and cutting the deck, deal a seven-row horizontal tableau with each of the last six rows overlapping the one above. The tableau is as follows: 1st row, eight cards face up; 2nd row, six cards face down on the middle six cards of the 1st row; 3rd row, six cards face up on the six above; 4th row, four cards face down on the middle four cards of the 3rd row; 5th row, four cards face up on the four above; 6th row, two cards face down on the middle two cards of the 5th row; 7th row, two cards face up on the two above. Place the remaining 20 cards face down as *stock*.

The newly dealt tableau has eight exposed cards on which you can play immediately; 12 cards face up on which you cannot play; and 12 cards face down—The Masked Twelve.

The Goal

The goal of the game is to play out all cards on the *foundations* in upward sequence by rank and suit.

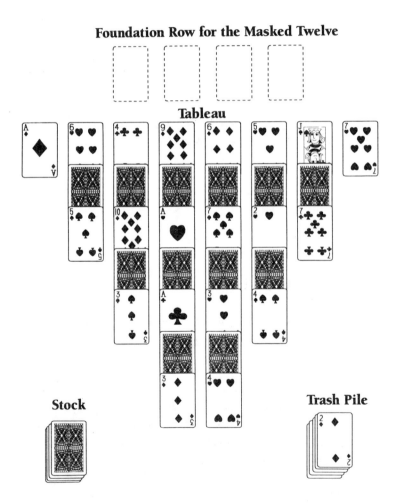

Foundation Row for the Masked Twelve

Tableau

Stock

Trash Pile

The Play

Play any aces exposed in the tableau to the foundations. *On foundation aces*, build upward sequences by rank and suit. On the exposed free cards in the tableau, build downward sequences by rank and in alternate colors. Within the tableau, you may move a card or sequence to another card as long as that card is one rank higher and a different color than the card or sequence being moved. When there is a space in the tableau—that is, fewer than seven vertical columns—you must play a king or a king-high sequence to fill it.

After you initially play whatever cards you can from the stock and tableau to the foundations and make whatever shifts possible in the tableau, you next can start turning the cards in the stock over one at a time and play them on the foundations, in the tableau, or face up on the *discard pile*, if unplayable. Thus you go through the stock one time only. Once you have exhausted the stock, you may still play from the discard pile, but you can play the top card only. Once you play that card, the one beneath it becomes available for play.

Continue playing in the manner described above until the game ends.

Game

You win the game if you play all cards to the foundations. Otherwise, you lose.

Lucky Thirteen

Lucky Thirteen presents a different *tableau* and requires a deck of 52 cards. The cards rank: ace (low) . . . king (high).

Beginning the Game

After shuffling and cutting the deck, deal a horizontal row of 13 cards face down. Next, on each of these cards, deal a second and third row of 13 cards each, face down, one at a time, from left to right. Finally, on the cards thus far laid out, deal a fourth row of 13 cards face up. This layout provides a tableau of 13 separate piles, each having four cards (three face down and one face up), for a total of 52 cards.

Foundation Row for the Lucky Thirteen

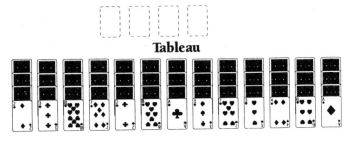

The Goal

The goal of the game is to play off all the cards on the four foundation aces in upward sequences by rank and suit. If you do not face an ace on the original layout or expose one by shifting cards within the tableau, the game ends because you cannot play further.

The Play

On the 13 exposed cards in the tableau, build downward sequences by rank and in alternate colors. Remove any aces from the tableau and place them face up in the *foundation* row. On the foundation aces, build upward sequences by rank and suit.

You may move a card or sequence from one tableau pile to another if the bottom card is one rank lower and a different color than the card to which you are playing it. When a space becomes available in the tableau, you may fill it only with a king or a king-high sequence. The pile from which you moved the king or king-high sequence now has a face-down card that may be turned face up and played, if possible.

Continue playing in the manner described above until the game ends.

Game

You win the game if you play all cards to the foundations.

Sham Battle

Sham Battle, which presents yet another type of *foundation/tableau* layout, requires a deck of 52 cards. The cards rank: ace (low) . . . king (high).

Beginning the Game

Separate the aces from the deck and position them as *foundation* aces in a vertical column in front of you, leaving ample space between them to build in upward sequence. Next, after shuffling and cutting the remaining 48 cards, deal six overlapping cards face up on each side of each ace. Build each six-card group from the ace outward so that the card farthest away from the ace is the top card. Thus, the tableau, or layout, exposes all 52 cards.

The Goal

The goal of the game is to play all cards on the foundation aces.

Tableau   Foundations   Tableau

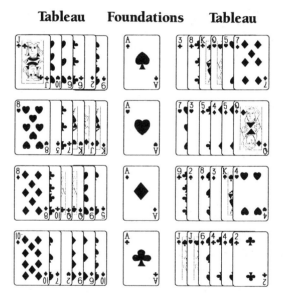

The Play

On the foundation aces, build upward sequences by rank and suit. On the outer end of each tableau row, play cards from one tableau row to another in downward sequence by rank, without regard to suit or color. You can move only one card at a time. When you clear a tableau row on either side of a foundation ace, you may fill the space with any card from the outer end of another tableau row. Continue the game as described above until you play all the cards on the foundation aces or until you can play no more cards to the foundation aces.

Game

You win the game if you play all the cards on the foundation aces.

Note: If you can clear one tableau row, you might possibly win; if you can clear two such rows, a win is probable; if you can clear three such rows, a win is almost certain.

Streets and Alleys ——————————

Streets and Alleys is a variation of Sham Battle. The two games differ as follows:

1. During the deal, leave a vertical space, or an alley, for the *foundation* aces in the middle of the table. Turn all 52 cards face up in 13 horizontal rows of four cards each. Build each four-card overlapping row away from the central space, or alley, so that the card farthest away from the ace is the top card. The completed *tableau* provides 7 four-card rows to the left of the alley and 6 four-card rows to the right of the alley.

2. As you expose aces in play, place them immediately in the alley, or central space, left for them during the deal.

Otherwise, the two games are the same.

Idiot's Delight ——————————

Idiot's Delight, which also requires a 52-card deck, presents another variation in *tableau* building. The cards rank: ace (low) . . . king (high).

Beginning the Game

After shuffling and cutting the deck, deal the tableau by turning a vertical column of nine cards face up, overlapping them from the top downwards. Next, turn a vertical column of eight cards face up to the right of the first column. Similarly, turn columns of seven, six, five, four, three, two, and one cards face up. Finally, turn the last seven cards of the deck face up horizontally as a *playing row* below the tableau. Thus, all 52 cards are exposed.

The Goal

The goal of the game is to play all cards to the foundation row.

Foundation Row for Idiot's Delight

Tableau for Idiot's Delight

Seven Card Playing Row

The Play

You can move one card at a time from the bottom of any vertical tableau pile. On the tableau, build downward sequences by rank and in alternate colors. As aces become available on the tableau or seven-card playing row, build upward sequences by rank and suit on the *foundations*, or aces. You may fill a space in the tableau with a card from the tableau or playing row. You do not have to play a card to the foundation row, but once you do, you cannot remove it. Similarly, if you play a card from the playing row to the tableau, you cannot return it to the playing row.

Continue the play until the game ends, which occurs when you play all the cards to the foundation row or when you can play no further from the playing row and tableau to the foundations.

Game

You win the game if you play all the cards on the foundation row.

Upside-Down Pyramid _____

The Upside-Down Pyramid, which introduces another type of *tableau*, requires two decks of cards. The cards rank: ace (low) . . . king (high).

Beginning the Game
After thoroughly shuffling two decks of cards and cutting them, lay out a tableau of 55 cards—all face up—as follows: From left to right, deal a ten-card top row; then from right to left, deal a nine-card row beneath the first row but slightly overlapping the cards above; then, in the same fashion, from left to right and then from right to left, deal out rows of eight, seven, six, five, four, three, two, and one cards. The completed tableau has ten horizontal rows, containing 55 cards. The remaining 49 cards are *stock*.

The Goal
The goal of the game is to play all 104 cards to the foundation row.

The Play
Only the exposed card in each horizontal row of the tableau is available for play. Within the tableau, you may build downward sequences by suit and in alternate colors on the exposed cards. You may shift a card or cards from one row to another so long as the card played to is one higher in rank and a different color. You may fill an empty space within the tableau only with a king or king-high sequence. As aces are exposed during play, move them above the tableau to form an eight-card *foundation* row, on which you must build upward sequences by rank and suit.

After you have made all possible plays within the tableau and moved any exposed aces to the foundation row, you then may turn the cards face up from the stock one at a time and play them to the foundation row or tableau. You may run through the stock only once.

Game
If you play all 104 cards on the foundation row, you win.

Tableau for Upside-Down Pyramid

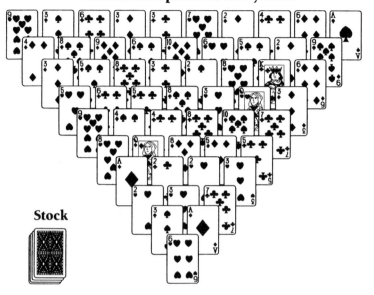

Financier

Financier is Solitaire with a different twist. Needed for the game are two decks of cards with the aces removed, providing a total of 96 cards. The cards rank: 2 (low) . . . king (high).

Beginning the Game
After thoroughly shuffling the cards and cutting them, lay out a *tableau* of three vertical columns, each containing eight cards face up but not overlapping. Leave sufficient horizontal space between the vertical columns so that you can eventually play on each card an upward sequence by suit. Ideally, all 2s should appear in column one; all 3s, in column two; and all 4s, in column three. Since the odds are against your dealing this ideal tableau, Financier challenges you not only to move through legitimate play all 2s, 3s, and 4s

to their appropriate columns, but also to play on each an upward sequence by suit. See the figure below.

Beneath the tableau, turn eight additional cards face up as a *playing row*. The remaining 64 cards are *stock*.

The Goal

The goal of the game is (a) to move the eight 2s, 3s, and 4s to their respective columns in the tableau, and (b) to build on each of the eight 2s, 3s, and 4s the upward-suit sequence designated in the figure below.

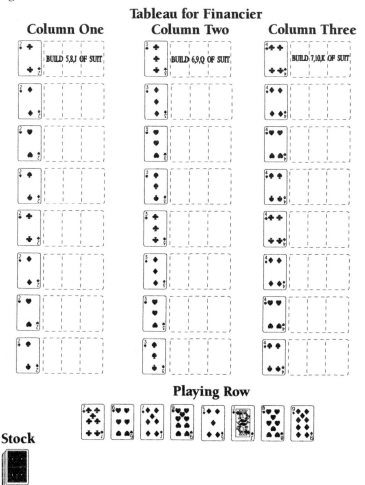

Tableau for Financier

Column One	Column Two	Column Three

Playing Row

Stock

The Play

On each 2 in the first column, build a 2, 5, 8, and jack sequence, by suit, with cards from the tableau or from the playing row below it. On each 3 in column two, build a 3, 6, 9, and queen sequence, by suit, in the same manner. On each 4 in column three, build a 4, 7, 10, king sequence, by suit, similarly. Once an empty space occurs in a tableau row, you must fill it immediately or as soon as possible with a card from another row in the tableau or from the playing row according to this scheme: Fill a space in the first column *only* with a 2; a space in the second column *only* with a 3; a space in the third column *only* with a 4.

After moving cards around within the tableau according to the rules above, you may move any 2s, 3s, or 4s from the playing row to empty spaces in the appropriate tableau columns. You also may move any card from the playing row to the 2s, 3s, and 4s in the tableau rows as long as it is the upward-suit sequence designated in the figure above.

When you can move no more cards around within the tableau and do not want to move any more cards from the playing row to the tableau, you may turn eight cards from the stock face up on the playing-row cards or spaces left empty through play. Overlap these rows vertically so that all cards are visible and easily read. You may not move cards from one playing row to another under any circumstances, even to fill spaces in the playing row.

As stated above, you cannot leave an empty space in a tableau row if there is an appropriate exposed card in the tableau or the playing row with which to fill it. If you move a card from the playing row to the tableau, the card beneath, if any, immediately becomes available for play. After all possible moves in the tableau and from the playing row to tableau have been made, you may deal out another eight cards on the playing row and resume play. Continue this procedure until you exhaust the stock.

Game

You win the game if you move all 2s, 3s, and 4s to their appropriate tableau columns, and if you are able to build the appropriate upward sequence by suit on each 2, 3, and 4, as in the figure above.

The Stops Group

Stops was the first game in which cards were used face down as "stops" to prevent playing out a suit in upward sequence. Thus, the goal of play, which was to build a suit in upward sequence, from ace to king, was thwarted only by a "stop" card.

Historically, the game seems to have made its debut in 1682, when many people became apprehensive about the appearance of Halley's comet. These people believed that the comet presaged the end of the world, which would put a stop to everything. Thus the "stops" in the game gently mocked these apprehensive believers.

The French called the game *Comète*, or Comet, and the English corrupted *Comète* to Commit. After changing the name to Commit, the English later added to it elements from the showdown game called Matrimony (see page 93). From the game of Matrimony, they borrowed the elements of marriage and intrigue and added them to Commit to form the popular game Pope Joan. In turn, they then eliminated the Pope, or diamond 7 or 9, to form the game of Newmarket, or Stops, which Americans renamed Boodle, Chicago, or Michigan.

Categorically, all such games are called "play-off games," and there are many variations, some of which have become children's games. Games specifically for children have been labelled by an age range.

Commit

Commit requires a deck of 51 cards (the 8 of diamonds is omitted) and two to eight players, although five or more are best. The cards rank: ace (low), 2, 3 . . . jack, queen, king (high).

Beginning the Game

The players draw or cut for low card (ace lowest) to determine first deal. The dealer gives each player one card at a time, in rotation from left to right, and places all odd cards left over face down as the stops hand.

The following schedule for dealing has been provided for the players' convenience. If two play, each player gets 20 cards, leaving 11 stops; if three play, each gets 14, leaving nine; if four play, each gets 11, leaving seven; if five play, each gets nine, leaving six; etc. An easier-to-remember schedule is that of dealing an extra hand for stops to the right of the dealer.

Ranking of Cards in Commit

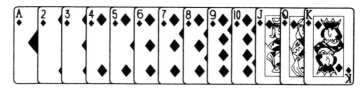

The Goal
The goal of the game is to be the first player to get rid of all your cards.

The Play
The player to the dealer's left leads any card she wishes, placing it face up on the table and playing on it all cards forming an upward sequence in the same suit. When she can no longer play, she says, "Without the 6," or whatever card she lacks. Then, in rotation from left to right, each player continues the sequence upwards or says "Without," adding whatever card she lacks. This routine continues until a king (a natural stop), the diamond 7, or some card concealed in the stops hand falls. Each person playing a king collects 1 chip from each player.

The person playing the stops card (a king, diamond seven, or the card just below the card from the stops hand) leads to the next sequence, and play continues until one person gets rid of all her cards. If a player holds the diamond 9, she may play that card whenever it is her turn to play. The play then passes to her left, and the next player may continue with the 10 of diamonds, jack of diamonds, and so forth. When a person plays the diamond 9, she collects 2 chips from each player.

Scoring

The first person to play all her cards wins the hand and the game. Any person holding a king at the end of play pays 1 chip to each player, and a person holding the diamond 9 at the end of play pays 2 chips to each player.

Fan-Tan

Fan-Tan, sometimes called "7s," requires three to eight players (although six or seven are best) and a deck of 52 cards. The cards rank: king (high), queen, jack, 10 . . . ace (low).

Beginning the Game

The players take an equal number of chips (beans, matchsticks, etc.), and each antes 1 chip before each deal. The players then draw or cut cards for first deal, with low draw winning. After the shuffle and cut, the dealer deals all the cards one at a time, in clockwise rotation, beginning at his left. Because the dealer can seldom give all players the same number of cards, those receiving one card less must ante another chip.

The Goal

The goal of each player is to play all his cards on sequences before any other person does so.

The Play

The player at the dealer's left has the first turn, and he must play a 7 if possible. If not possible, he puts 1 chip in the pool, and it becomes the next person's turn to play a 7. A person can always play a 7, and, as the game progresses, the 7s are laid out side by side in the middle of the table, each forming a base for the play of other cards of the same suit. Once a 7 appears on the table, the next player may play the 6 or 8 of the same suit. Similarly, the next player may play the 5 or 9 of the same suit, and so forth. Each person may play only one card per turn at play, and the game ends when one person plays all of his cards.

Settling Up

When a person plays his last card, he wins the hand and the game. The other players put 1 chip into the pool for each of their unplayed cards. The winner then claims the entire pool. A scorekeeper can keep score with a pencil and paper.

Penalties

If a person fails to play when able to do so, he forfeits 3 chips to the pool. If he fails to play a 7 when able to do so, he forfeits 5 chips to the holder(s) of the matching 6 and/or 8; however, a player need not play a 7 if he has another card he can and does play.

Variations

Some Fan-Tan enthusiasts prefer using a 60-card deck, one with cards containing 11 and 12 pips, because the deck is more likely to divide evenly on a deal to a larger number of players. When players use the 60-card deck, 8s and not 7s are used to begin play.

Original Fan-Tan

Original Fan-Tan differs from the present-day basic game in the following respects:

1. The player to the dealer's left leads *any card* she chooses, not necessarily a 7, and each player, in turn, must either play the next-highest card of the same suit on it or pay 1 chip to the pool. After the king is reached, the players then continue to build on the same sequence from the ace to the first card played in the sequence. The person completing the sequence then leads to the next sequence, playing any card she chooses.

2. A player cannot begin a new sequence until the one being played to is completed.

Note: To gain the right to lead to the second or a subsequent sequence, a player should lead the higher of two adjacent, or touching, cards to a new sequence. For example, if she holds an 8 and 9 in any suit, she should lead the 9, which will make her 8 the last card played to the sequence, thus assuring her the lead to the next sequence.

Card Games for Children and the Young at Heart

I Doubt It

This is a fast and funny game that tests players' ingenuity and ability to bluff. Three to six players require a full deck of 52 cards; seven to twelve players require two full decks. The cards function by rank only; thus, there are no distinctions between suits. The cards rank: ace (high), king, queen, jack, 10 . . . 2 (low).

Ranking of Cards in I Doubt It

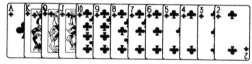

Beginning the Game

In the draw or cut for first deal, high cut wins. After the shuffle and cut, the dealer gives each player two or three cards at a time, in clockwise rotation, starting at his left. As the deal draws to a close, he gives each person one card at a time so that the difference in the number of cards held by the players never exceeds one. Thus, some players will hold one card more than the others.

The Goal

The goal of the game is for the player to get rid of all his cards by playing one to four cards of a required rank face down at his turn to play or by playing cards alleged or purported to be of such a rank.

The Play

The person to the dealer's left starts the game by playing one to four cards face down on the table and announcing the number of aces he allegedly has face down. Without delay, the next person, in turn, must play one to four cards face down of the next-lowest rank

88

(kings) and similarly announce them. Thus the play moves one rank downwards with each turn at play until the deuces are reached, whereupon the next person begins with aces and thus again initiates the downward movement. (Some players prefer letting the first player lead cards of any rank and then going to the next lower or higher rank, as agreed to at the beginning of play; the direction of play does not matter so long as the play is circular.) This procedure continues until one person plays, or gets rid of, all his cards.

As stated above, the cards played and announced by a person need not be what they are announced or purported to be, and at any time another person may say, "I doubt it." If so doubted, the player of those cards turns them face up. If the cards are not what they were announced to be in whole or in part, the person playing them must pick up all the cards on the table and add them to his hand. In this case, the doubter leads to the next trick. However, if the cards are what they were announced to be, the doubter must pick up all the cards on the table and add them to his hand. In this case, the next person in rotation leads to the next trick.

The person saying "I doubt it" must do so after the player announces the rank or alleged rank of the cards but before the player actually places them on the table. If several players call out, "I doubt it," at the same time, the one sitting closest to the player's left wins the right to challenge. Otherwise, the first person to say "I doubt it" wins the right to challenge.

Play thus continues until one person gets rid of all his cards, which ends play.

Note: It is acceptable for a person to say "I doubt it" in order to get the cards just played and announced so that he can build up a set of three or four cards of one rank. Doing so will equip him with a doubt-safe play. An accumulation of doubt-safe plays is very desirable as the game draws towards a close.

Settling Up

The players may regard each deal as a game, or they may play to 100 or 200 points, as agreed to at the beginning of play. If game is 100 or 200 points, any player may record the scores with pencil and paper. In the latter case, the winner collects the difference between his and the other players' scores.

Crazy 8s _____

This game, which is variously known as Crazy 7s, 8s, Jacks, etc., depending on the wild card named, requires two to four players and a 52-card deck. The cards rank: king (high), queen, jack, 10 . . . ace (low).

Beginning the Game
The players draw or cut cards for partners, if four play, and for first deal. High cuts play low cuts, and highest cut wins first deal. After the shuffle and cut in a two-hand game, the dealer gives each player seven cards, one at a time, in rotation to the left; in a three- or four-hand game, the dealer gives each player five cards. When finished, the dealer puts the stock face down in the middle of the table and turns the top card face up beside the stock as the *starter card* of the *talon*, or pile of played cards.

The Goal
The goal of the game is to be the first person to get rid of all one's cards by playing them to the talon.

The Play
The opponent (in a two-hand game) or the person sitting to the dealer's left (in a three- or four-hand game) must play to the starter card a card of the same suit or rank. Each person in turn continues to play a card of the same suit or rank to the top card of the talon. If she cannot do so, she must draw cards from the stock until she can play. A player may, however, draw cards from the stock even is she is able to play. Some players will do so to avoid having to play an 8, which is a wild card.

All 8s are wild, and any person may play an 8 to the talon and thereby win the right to name a new *suit* only, never a rank. She may play the 8 even if she is able to play a card of the same suit or rank. The next person, in turn, must play a card of the suit just named or play another 8.

If the stock becomes exhausted and a person cannot play to the talon, she passes and the next person in turn may play or pass. However, no one may pass if she holds a playable card. If the stock is exhausted and no one can play to the talon, the game ends in a *block*. If a block occurs and it is found to be a false block, or one that occurred because someone did not play a playable card, that person becomes barred from winning and play continues until the game ends or until a real block occurs.

In a two- or three-hand game, the play comes to an end when one of the players gets rid of her last card. In a four-handed game, play ends only when both players of a partnership get rid of their cards.

Scoring

The player or partnership that gets rid of their cards wins the hand and the game.

Many Crazy 8s enthusiasts prefer playing a longer game and score points for the unplayed cards in their opponents' hands according to this schedule: 50 points for each 8; 10 points for each face card; the pip, or index, value for each 10 . . . 2; 1 point for each ace.

If the game ends in a block, the player or partnership with the lowest total scores the difference between their and their opponents' scores. If a tie occurs in a three-hand game, the tied players divide the points earned.

A scorekeeper records a cumulative tally for each player at the end of each hand, and the first player or partnership to reach 100 points scores out and wins an additional 100 points for game.

Remedies and Penalties

If the dealer exposes a card during the deal, she must deal a new hand. However, if a person holds the wrong number of cards and she or another person has played to the starter card before the misdeal becomes known, she may draw cards from the stock to correct her card count. If she has too many cards, she must spread her cards face down on the table and let the opponent draw cards from the face-down hand to correct the card count.

Playing the Ponies _____

Playing the Ponies requires any number of persons (five to ten being best) and one deck of cards. The cards rank: ace (high), king, queen, jack, 10 . . . 2 (low). The suits rank: hearts (high), diamonds, clubs, and spades (low).

Beginning the Game

The players bid at auction for the right to be the dealer–banker. The highest bidder wins, and he uses the amount of his bid and accumulated wins as a pool from which to pay his losses, if any. The dealer–banker cannot lose beyond the limit of his pool.

The players use chips (beans, matchsticks, etc.) to place their bets on the layout. There are two types of bets: (1) even money, which is made by placing chips on black or red to win and which is won if the pony of the chosen color crosses the finish line first; (2) the color of the pony and an odds column. The dealer usually sets a bet limit.

After the shuffle and cut, the dealer "burns" the bottom card of the deck by turning it face up to the card above it and prepares to deal.

The layout of the racecourse is below.

The Goal

The goal of the game is to place a bet on the winning pony.

Racecourse for Playing the Ponies

BLACK		RED		
2 to 1	5 to 1	10 to 1	7 to 1	2 to 1
PONY	PONY	PONY	PONY	PONY

The Play

The dealer begins the play by turning one card face up beneath each of the five ponies (represented by a coin, checker, or some other item). High card moves its pony to the bottom line above it. Ties are broken by the rank of suits. The dealer then turns five more cards face up as he did above, and this continues until one of the ponies crosses the line. It takes only two moves for a pony in a 2-to-1 lane to win.

Settling Up

The dealer pays even-odds as indicated by the board to players who pick the winner by color, and he pays at the odds given to the winner. He then collects all other bets.

Matrimony ⸺

This game dates back to the 1500s, when face cards or combinations of face cards were regarded as personifications of royalty and other persons of power and influence. The king and queen represented matrimony; the queen and knave (jack), intrigue; the king and knave, confederacy; and the ace represented the merchant class, whose increasing wealth and power were rising.

Today, Matrimony requires a 52-card deck or a deck with some of its lower-ranking cards stripped from it to increase the odds for more-frequent wins. The game also requires the layout below, which may be made of paper or cardboard. Any number of persons can play.

Layout for Matrimony Board

MATRIMONY	INTRIGUE	CONFEDERACY	PAIR	BEST

Beginning the Game

To get the game under way, the players draw or cut cards to determine the first dealer–banker. High draw wins. The dealer then places the number of chips he is willing to wager on each of the above categories, and each player in rotation to the left places the same or smaller wager on one or, perhaps, two categories. Following the wager episode and the shuffle and cut, the dealer then gives each person two cards: one face down and one face up.

The Showdown
If a player gets the ace of diamonds face up, which is *Best*, he takes all the chips from the Best compartment of the layout. If the ace of diamonds does not appear face up, the chips remain on the layout until an ace of diamonds does appear face up in a later deal.

All the players then turn their hole cards face up. If a player holds any king and queen, he takes the chips from the Matrimony compartment. If a player holds any queen and jack, he takes the chips from Intrigue. If a player holds any king and jack, he takes the chips from Confederacy. If a player holds the highest pair, he takes the chips from Pair. In the event of a tie, the player sitting closest to the dealer's left wins.

The deal passes to the left at the end of each hand, and the new dealer–banker places his wager on each compartment so that the other players can place their wagers as above. While each hand is a game, a time limit is usually set for those wishing a longer session.

What the Terms Mean

Around the Corner: A phrase used to describe sequences, or runs, built around the corner, such as queen, king, ace, deuce (2), 3, 4, 5, 6, 7, 8, 9, 10, and jack.

Ante: Placing a certain amount of money on the table as a declaration of interest in playing the upcoming hand. In some games, only the dealer antes; in other games, all players ante.

Bid: A declaration to win/take a certain number of tricks or points in a hand of play.

Book: The number of tricks a person/team must take in Whist before subsequent tricks have value. In Whist, book is six points.

Denomination: The rank of a card, such as 2, 3, 4, etc.

Deuce: A 2 of any suit. Deuce and 2 are interchangeable terms.

Dummy: A hand that is not played by the person to whom it was dealt. Such a hand is played by that person's partner.

Face Card: A jack, queen, or king.

Follow Suit: Playing a card of the same suit that led the trick.

Lead: The right to lead or the act of leading the first card to a trick.

Meld: Any scoring combination of cards announced, shown, or played; it refers to combinations of three of a kind and/or three or more cards in sequence.

Pip Value: The counting value of a card. For example, in most games the counting value of 3 is 3, etc. In Black Jack, however, an ace has a counting value of 1 or 11.

Renege: To fail to follow suit when able to do so.

Revoke: To fail to play as required by the rules of the game. A revoke can mean the same thing as a renege, but it usually has a broader meaning and covers the violation of any rule of the game.

Sweep: Generally means winning/taking every trick in a hand of play. In Cassino, a sweep is taking all the cards on the table in one play.

Tricks: The cards taken/won in one round of play.

Trump Suit: The suit that is especially privileged to win over the cards of the other suits. For example, if diamonds are the trump suit, any diamond can win over any card of any other suit. Each game has its own process for selecting a trump suit.

Widow: A group of cards dealt separately in their own pile apart from the players' hands. In some games such as Hearts, the widow consists of the undealt portion of the deck and is taken by the winner of the first trick.

Wild Cards: Cards named by the dealer as wild before the deal. The holder of such cards may give any value to them that he or she chooses.

Index

All Fours Group, 12–16
Auction Pitch, 15–16
Auld Lang Syne, 68–69
Baseball, 33
Basic Poker, 21–27
Basic Rummy, 5–7
Bierspiel, 48
Black Jack, 34–37
Black Jack Hearts, 61
Black Lady, 64–65
Bluff Poker, 27–28
Bold Stand, 49
Bozenkill Rummy, 8
Brag, 21
Buck Euchre, 44
Call-Ace Euchre, 45
Card games, reasons for
    playing, 4
Card terms, 94–96
Cassino, 54–57
Cassino Group, 54–58
Children's card games,
    88–94
Commit, 84–86
Contract Whist, 20
Crazy 8s, 90–91
Deuces Wild, 30
Double pool, 49
Draw Poker, 28–29
Euchre, 38–42
Euchre Group, 38–53
Fan-Tan, 86–87
Favorite Whist, 19
Financier, 81–83
Firing Squad, 66–68
Five-Card Loo, 51

Five-Card Stud, 31–32
French Ruff, 38
Gate card, 37
Gin Rummy, 9–11
Good Measure, 70–71
Hearts, 59–61
Hearts Group, 59–65
High-Low Poker, 33
Idiot's Delight, 78–79
I Doubt It, 88–89
Irish Loo, 51
Jackpots, 29
Jambone, 42–43
Jamboree, 43
Klondike, 72–73
Laps, 42
Loo, 49–51
Lowball, 31
Lucky Thirteen, 75–76
Masked Twelve, 73–75
Matrimony, 84, 93–94
Mexican Stud, 32
Michigan Rummy, 8
Napolean, 51–53
Original Fan-Tan, 87
Pass and Out, 29
Patience Group, 66–83
Playing the Ponies, 91–93
"Play-Off Games," 84–87
Poker Group, 20–33
Pope Joan, 84
Port card, 37
Progressive Draw Poker,
    29
Prussian Whist, 19
Railroad Euchre, 44

Rams, 38, 45–47
Red Jack Hearts, 61
Royal Cassino, 57
Royal Draw Cassino, 58
Rummy Group, 5–11
Seven-Card Stud, 32–33
7s, 86–87
Seven-Up, 12–15
Sham Battle, 76–78
Showdown Games Group,
    34–37
Showdown Rummy, 8
Six-Hand Euchre, 43
Simple Pool, 49
Slams, 42
Solitaire Group, 66–83
Spade Cassino, 58
Spanish Monte, 37
Spit in the Ocean, 30
Stops Group, 84–87
Straight Pitch, 16
Straight Poker, 27–28
Streets and Alleys, 78
Suite Value Whist, 19
Three-Hand Euchre, 43
Three-Hand Whist,
    19–20
3s in the Corner, 69–70
Two-Hand Euchre, 43
Two-Hand Whist, 20
Two-Ten-Jack, 62–63
Upside-Down Pyramid,
    80–81
Whist, 17–19
Whist Group, 17–20
Wild Widow, 30